LET US PRAY:
474 PROPHETIC PRAYERS

By
BISHOP (DR). ISRAEL ADE-AJALA

First Edition

Copyright ©2023 Israel Ade-Ajala
All rights reserved.

Published by The Lighthouse books, Agape Inc.

All rights reserved. No part of this publication may be used or reproduced in any manner whatsoever without the written permission except in the case of brief quotations embedded in critical articles and reviews.

Requests for permission should be addressed to the Lighthouse Books Editor at editor@thelighthousebooks.com

For more information regarding permission, write to:
The Lighthouse Books, 13721 E. Rice Pl, Aurora,
CO 80015.

Scripture quotations are from the New King James Version marked NKJV except otherwise stated.

All rights reserved. Scripture quotations marked KJV are taken from the Holy Bible, King James Version®. All rights reserved. Scripture quotations marked NLT are taken from the Holy Bible, New Living Translation®. All rights reserved. Scripture quotations marked ESV are taken from the Holy Bible, English Standard Version®. All rights reserved. Scripture quotations marked God's Word Translation are taken from the Holy Bible, God's Word Translation®. All rights reserved. Scripture quotations marked NASB are taken from the Holy Bible, New American Standard Bible®. All rights reserved. Scripture quotations marked CEV are taken from the Holy Bible, Contemporary English Version®. All rights reserved. Scripture quotations marked CEB are taken from the Holy Bible, The Common English Bible® version. All rights reserved. Scripture quotations marked TLB are taken from the Holy Bible, The Living Bible® version. All rights reserved. Scripture quotations marked TPT are taken from the Holy Bible, The Passion Translation®. All rights reserved. Scripture quotations marked AMPC are taken from the Holy Bible, Amplified Bible Classic Edition®. All rights reserved. Scripture quotations marked BBE are taken from the Holy Bible, The Bible in Basic English®. All rights reserved. Scripture quotations marked "Message" are taken from the Holy Bible, The Bible in Contemporary Language®. All rights reserved. Scripture quotations marked Berean Study Bible are taken from the Holy Bible, Berean Study Bible®. All rights reserved.

ISBN: 978-1-950320-61-5 [Paperback]
ISBN: 978-1-950320-58-5 [Digital]

Visit us at:
www.thelighthousebooks.com
Printed in the USA

Dedication

To my wife Adeola and my children, Holly, Adebowale and Donald Ajala. For all your support over the years. Finally to my Lord and Savior Jesus Christ. To Him be glory and honor forever.

Words of Wisdom

When I call to remembrance the genuine faith that is in you, which dwelt first in your grandmother Lois and your mother Eunice, and I am persuaded is in you also."

2 Timothy 1: 5 (NKJV)

The testimony of a grandmother, the mother of the author; a model of a prayerful woman.

This prayer book is a must have for every serious believer who want to catch the fire of intercessory prayer and passion for praying. This book will help you to pray and aid you to develop the must have habits of prayer. Every prayer in this book is backed up by scriptures. This is how we must pray. God honors such prayers that remind HIM of HIS Word. - Pray until your joy is full.

To all believers, if God is your Father, then call home!

This prayer book will help you to have constant victories, undeniable breakthroughs and tangible testimonies.

I developed the passion for prayer and positive declaration when I was 3 years old. I was told the story of my early childhood that I was late to start walking. I didn't start walking until I was 3 years old. There was this uncle of mine who started calling me "the crawler." With prayer, I rejected that name. God honored my little faith and confession, and I started walking. This made me to be outspoken when it comes to talking and declaring what God says about me, not what man says about me.

It is important to state that there is this belief that the power of darkness and witchcrafts gather to destroy people's destiny at midnight. Realizing this belief, I made up my mind that I will operate in the spirit realm, in prayers, during that same hour to pray for my children (biological, spiritual, adopted). I started this practice years ago and I am thankful to God for His grace and strength. It is important for parents to model the habit of praying to their children. Don't just tell them to pray, let them see you pray. They will follow your example faster than your advice!

Reading God's Word helps me to pray. I am a lover of God's word, and that has helped me in my prayer life. I encourage everyone to fall in love with the word of God and to also make sure that the children fall in love with the Word of God early in life. I introduced all my children to the Word of God early and often. Reading, studying, memorizing and obeying the Word of God is very important as we develop the lifestyle of prayer. Years ago, shortly after my husband passed, I perceived a spiritual attack looming, and my children and I started praying in our living room at night, declaring the judgment of the Lord upon the works of satan. We called the sword of the Lord to cut into pieces all the agents of darkness. In the morning, we physically saw dead, dismembered cats outside of our house. I have seen the Lord answer prayers in mysterious way. Sometimes the answer to your prayers will come immediately, other times the answers will come suddenly. Yet, other times, it might take time to receive your answers. But one thing I know is that the Lord answers prayers. Don't stop praying!

I understood by experience that you can pray for someone in another part of the world and that person will feel your prayer and the Lord will do what you requested. There is power in the sent Word. Pray for others, whether they are far or near – send the word. This can be achieved if you get a prayer partner. I have a prayer partner that I pray with every week. Praying partners help you become accountable to one another. Being accountable and having an accountability partner is a good way of life. If you want to go fast, they say, go alone, but if you want to go far, go with others. This is a good word to live by in your prayer life. I encourage everyone to have a prayer partner.

One of my beloved prayer scriptures is one of the shortest verses in the bible, "Pray without ceasing." I took that literally. Instead of engaging in idle talk, I just developed the habit of talking to God. I really love talking to God because it makes me happy and gives me joy. This prayer book will help you accomplish that. For me, you don't have to encourage me to pray because I have seen prayer turn things around for me and for the people that I've prayed for. I remember when I was back in Nigeria, I declared it by faith that I will live the latter part of my life in the United States of America, I had no idea how it would happen. The Lord honored that prayer. I also prayed that all my children must know and serve God. The Lord honored that prayer also. Don't tell me that prayer doesn't work!

In fact, there is an event in my life that I remember very clearly. When I was raising my children in Nigeria, after dinner, I will tell them good night. But at midnight, I will wake up and start praying. But, my son, Bishop Israel will be peeping through the doors to see what I was doing. And, not too long, I saw him pick up this same habit of mine. And, he has never stopped since then.

One thing you must know is this: praying for others, even when you have your own needs, is powerful. I grew up praying for other people. Asking God to provide for them even when I didn't have enough to provide for my children. Every time, without fail, God, will suddenly open His windows and pour out His blessings by meeting our needs. Praying to God is what I do. It is what Bishop Israel does. Moreover, the Bible is the best and only place you can go to if you don't know how to pray and what to pray for. You can draw near to God when you pray. You can hear Him when you pray. I am a living testimony of this. I prayed and prayed and prayed and still praying and the Lord answered and is still answering me.

- Grandma Comfort Ajala.
[Mother of the Author of 'Let Us Pray']

Contents

Foreword 1

Thanksgiving 3

Dedication 10

Deliverance 14

Spiritual Warfare 17

The Church 54

Family 78

Protection 88

Divine Healing 99

Victory 102

Blessing 111

Pastors 121

Success 133

Foreword

The secret of my victories is prayer. The unrestricted access to God is my most cherished privilege. I was fortunate to know earlier in my life that prayer changes things, that prayer gives us strength, and that prayer helps us to have fellowship with God.

I am a product of a praying mother. It was not the spankings of my mother that changed me, it was her prayers. Keep praying, it makes all the difference.

Jesus gave us the pattern of prayer in the book of Matthew chapter 6, in verses 6 - 9, Jesus taught us that praying is a relationship-based communication:

"But you, when you pray, go into your room, and when you have shut your door, pray to **your Father** *who is in the secret place; and* **your Father** *who sees in secret will reward you openly. And when you pray, do not use vain repetitions as the heathen do. For they think that they will be heard for their many words. "Therefore, do not be like them. For* **your Father** *knows the things you have need of before you ask Him. In this manner, therefore, pray:* **Our Father** *in heaven, Hallowed be Your name."* (Matthew 6:6-9 NKJV)

When you pray, pray to your Father in the name of the Son, Jesus. The Father will honor every prayer prayed in this manner.

"And in that day you will ask Me nothing. Most assuredly, I say to you, whatever you **ask the Father in My name He will give you."** (John 16:23 NKJV)

As you pray to the Father in the name of His Son, Jesus, pray in faith believing that you have what you asked for. Do not doubt that you've received your petition.

"...ask in faith, with no doubting, for he who doubts is like a wave of the sea driven and tossed by the wind. For let not that man suppose that he will receive anything from the Lord; he is a double-minded man, unstable in all his ways." (James 1:6-8 NKJV)

Every prayer in this prayer book is scripture based. Pray for yourself, your children, your spouse, your parents, your friends, your pastors and more.

Receive answers to all your prayers. Let Us Pray!

Bishop Israel Ade-Ajala

Thanksgiving

THANKSGIVING GIVES YOU ACCESS TO THE PRESENCE OF GOD. IF YOU CAN THINK, YOU WILL SEE THAT THERE ARE A MULTITUDE OF REASONS TO BE THANKFUL TO GOD FOR ALL HE HAS DONE FOR YOU. IN EVERYTHING AND FOR EVERYTHING GIVE THANKS (1 THESSALONIANS 5:18). WHEN YOU ARE THANKFUL, YOU ARE IN THE WILL OF GOD.

EVERY TIME THAT GOD IS FAITHFUL, YOU MUST BE THANKFUL. OH, GIVE THANKS TO THE LORD, FOR HE IS GOOD! FOR HIS MERCY ENDURES FOREVER. (PSALMS 136:1) LET US PRAY!

1. *Psalms 31:21 "Praise the Lord, for he has shown me the wonders of his unfailing love. He kept me safe when my city was under attack." (NLT).*

   Father, I praise you for keeping me, my family, my church, and all that surrounds me safe from January to December. Thank you for keeping us safe from the attacks of the enemies.

2. *Psalms 75:1 "Our God, we thank you for being so near to us! Everyone celebrates your wonderful deeds." (CEV).*

   Father, we thank you for your blessings in our lives, homes, jobs, businesses, and church. Thank you for providing our needs for our new church building!

3. *Romans 5:7-8 "For scarcely for a righteous man will one die; yet perhaps for a good man someone would even dare to die. But God demonstrates His own love toward us, in that while we were still sinners, Christ died for us." (NKJV).*

   My Lord and My King, I thank You for paying the price for me on the cross. Thank you, for paying my debt on Calvary.

4. *Luke 10:19 "See what I've given you? Safe passage as you walk on snakes and scorpions, and protection from every assault of the Enemy. No one can put a hand on you!" (Message).*

   Father, I praise you for keeping me, my family, my pastors, my church and all that surround me safe since January. Thank you for keeping us safe from the attacks of the enemies and for granting us victory on every side, in the name of Jesus!

5. *Psalms 106:1 "Praise the Lord! Give thanks to The Lord because He is good, because His faithful love endures forever." (CEB).*

   Let us thank God for all that He has been doing for us at our church and give Him praise.

6. *Proverbs 24:16 "No matter how many times you trip them up, God–loyal people don't stay down long; Soon they're up on their feet, while the wicked end up flat on their faces." (Message).*

   Father, thank you for keeping us on our feet, despite all the plans of the wicked. Thank you for keeping us standing with proof of your love and faithfulness.

7. Psalms 75:4-5 "You tell every bragger, 'Stop bragging!' And to the wicked you say, 'Don't boast of your power! Stop bragging! Quit telling me how great you are.'" (CEV).

Father, thank you for silencing every bragger against our destiny and the destiny of our church. Father, thank you for lifting us up amid opposition and hate. Thank you for allowing us to keep enjoying your love and mercy in the name of JESUS!

8. Matthew 10:1 "And when He had called His twelve disciples to Him, He gave them power over unclean spirits, to cast them out, and to heal all kinds of sickness and all kinds of disease." (NKJV).

Lord, we thank you for all that you are doing at our church. Father, reposition our church as a ministry, and use this church to destroy the satanic kingdom in this nation and all over the world in the name of Jesus!

9. Psalms 75:1 "Our God, we thank you for being so near to us! Everyone celebrates your wonderful deeds." (CEV).

Father, we thank you for your blessings in our lives, children, homes, jobs, businesses and church. Thank you for providing for our needs and for our church for these past years!

10. Psalms 26:7 "Singing God-songs at the top of my lungs, telling God stories." (Message).

Father, I declare that I will sing songs of thanksgiving, and I will tell of all your wonders in my life. My time to share testimonies has finally come in the name of Jesus!

11. Revelation 13:8 *And all the people who belong to this world worshiped the beast. They are the ones whose names were not written (Blotted Out) in the Book of Life that belongs to the Lamb who was slaughtered before the world was made. (NLT). Revelation 13:8 All who dwell on the earth will worship him. Those, whose names have not been written in the Book of Life of the Lamb, slain from the foundation of the world. (NKJV).*

Father, I thank you for the Lamb of God that was slain from the foundation of the world.

12. Psalms 45:11 *" So the King will greatly desire your beauty; Because He is your Lord, worship Him. (NKJV).*

Father, we thank you because of your beauty in our lives, in our homes, in our children, in our finances, and over our works. We are the envy of your blessing and favor and the World sees it! We celebrate your goodness.

13. Psalms 144:1 1 *"Praise the LORD, who is my rock. He trains my hands for war and gives my fingers skill for battle." (NLT).*

Father, we thank you for giving us victory in every battle we have fought this year. Thank you for making us winners and not losers in the name of Jesus.

14. Judges 5:20 *"The stars fought from heaven. The stars in their orbits fought against Sisera." (NLT).*

Father, thank you for fighting our battles and giving us victory. We praise you for defeating the Sisera of COVID-19 and other ravaging diseases. Lord, we praise you for protecting us from what is killing others. We confidently say, "We lost no one to COVID-19!"

15. *1 Chronicles 29:11 "Yours, O Lord, is the greatness, The power and the glory, The victory and the majesty; For all that is in heaven and in earth is Yours; Yours is the kingdom, O Lord, And You are exalted as head over all." (NKJV).*

Father, we sincerely acknowledge, you are God that rules supreme in our affairs, thank you for the testimonies of your faithfulness, in our corporate and individual lives.

16. *Philippians 2:13 "For it is God who works in you both to will and to do for His good pleasure." (NKJV).*

Thank you Father for Your Grace and mercy; which enrolled me among the redeemed, the blessed, and the sanctified.

17. *Psalms 127: 2 "It is vain for you to rise up early, to sit up late, to eat the bread of sorrows; For so He gives His beloved sleep."*

Heavenly Father, here at this church, we thank you for granting us rest from toiling and laboring and replacing labor with your favor. Father, thank you for granting us the wisdom to achieve divine balance in all our endeavors and for releasing your peace that surpasses all understanding in Jesus' name.

18. *Psalms 102:2-5 "Praise the Lord, my soul, and forget not all his benefits; who forgives all your sins and heals all your diseases, who redeems your life from the pit, and crowns you with love and compassion; who satisfies your desires with good things so that your youth is renewed like the eagle's. (KJV).*

Father, we cannot forget the way you forgive us all for our sins and redeem us from the jaw of death. Take your glory Lord, over our senior pastor. Receive your praise Lord, over every member of this church family. Take your glory Lord.

19. 1 Corinthians 15:57 "But thanks be to God! He gives us the victory through our Lord Jesus Christ." (NIV).

Father, in the name of Jesus, thank you for giving us victory constantly at our church over all the plans & works of the enemy. Thank you, Jesus!

20. Numbers 6: 24-26 "May the Lord bless you and protect you. May the Lord smile on you and be gracious to you. May the Lord show you his favor and give you his peace." (NLT).

Father, we thank you that you are the God of peace. We thank you that even when the earth is trembling, we can be still and know you are God. Nothing can separate us from You. We praise you for your protection and favor. As we sit in your presence and focus our hearts and minds on you, give us your perfect peace. We trust that no matter what, you will guide us, protect us, and be gracious toward us.

21. Romans 15:13 "Now may the God of hope fill you with all joy and peace in believing, that you may abound in hope by the power of the Holy spirit." (NKJV).

Father, we rejoice today because you never change. You are the same yesterday, today, and tomorrow. We thank you that your Holy Spirit is filling our family right now with unspeakable joy and peace that passes all understanding.

22. 2 *Corinthians 9:15 "Thanks be to God for His indescribable gifts." (NKJV).*

Father, thank You for this church. Thank you for increasing your church. Thank you for the wonder working Word of life in this church.

Dedication

Daily dedicating oneself to the Lord is a great practice. Prayer of dedication is to present oneself to the Lord daily, monthly or yearly. It is a good thing to present your family, children, business and yourself to the lord. Romans 12: 1 says, "I beseech you therefore, brethren, by the mercies of God, that you present your bodies a living sacrifice, holy, acceptable to God which is your reasonable service. Let us pray!

23. *Job 34: 32 "So why don't you simply confess to God? Say, 'I sinned, but I'll sin no more. Teach me to see what I still don't see. Whatever evil I've done, I'll do it no more.'" (Message).*

Father, I confess and repent in totality, every sin that gave Satan and his demons entrance into my life, my business, and my finances in the name of Jesus; and I cast them out of my life in the name of Jesus.

24. *1 Samuel 28:15 "Why have you disturbed me by bringing me back?" Samuel asked Saul. "Because I am in deep trouble," he replied. "The Philistines are at war with us, and God has left me and won't reply by prophets or dreams; so, I have called for you to ask you what to do." (NLT).*

Father, cleanse me and purge me of anything and everything that can make me lose Your glorious presence. Lord, make Your presence more real to me day by day.

25. Daniel 10:19 *"And he said, "O man greatly beloved, fear not! Peace be to you; be strong, yes, be strong!" So when he spoke to me, I was strengthened, and I said, "Let My Lord speak, for you have strengthened me." (NKJV).*

Father, speak to me. Speak to my health, my finances, my marriage, my ministry, my career, my business, my children, my home, and my life. Strengthen me in the name of Jesus. Don't let me fall apart in the name of Jesus.

26. Psalms 138:8 *"You keep every promise you've ever made to me! Since your love for me is constant and endless, I ask you, Lord, to finish every good thing that you've begun in me!" (Passion).*

Father, finish every good thing you've begun in my life, home, career, finances, children, and business in the name of Jesus. Let the people see that your hand is upon my life and confess it in the name of Jesus.

27. Matthew 6:31 33 *"Therefore do not worry, saying, 'What shall we eat?' or 'What shall we drink?' or 'What shall we wear?' 32 For after all these things the Gentiles seek. For your heavenly Father knows that you need all these things. 33 But seek first the kingdom of God and His righteousness, and all these things shall be added to you." (NKJV).*

Father, I give you the first place and the full place in my business and in my career. I declare that I will serve you Oh Lord with the proceeds from my business faithfully, withholding nothing from you Oh Lord!

28. <u>Acts 6:7</u> *"And the word of God increased; and the number of the disciples multiplied in Jerusalem greatly; and a great company of the priests were obedient to the faith." (KJV).*

Father, let the knowledge of your word grow in us as individuals. Let it grow in our families and in our church family so that we will continue to affect our neighborhoods, our city, state and our nation for God, in the mighty name of Jesus Christ.

29. *2 Chronicles 7:14 "If My people who are called by My name will humble themselves, and pray and seek My face, and turn from their wicked ways, then I will hear from heaven, and will forgive their sin and heal their land." (NKJV).*

Father, as we pray and seek your face today, help us to turn from our wicked ways. Help us to be kind to one another the way we should. Forgive us for all sins and heal our land in the mighty name of Jesus Christ.

30. *1 Thessalonians 5:18 "In everything, give thanks; for this is the will of God in Christ Jesus for you." (NKJV).*

Thank you, Lord, for the blessings you have bestowed on our lives, children, home, jobs, businesses, and church. Father, thank you for providing us with more than we could ever have imagined in our homes and for our church.

31. *Psalms 86:12 "I will praise You, O Lord my God, with all my heart, And I will glorify your name forevermore." (NKJV).*

Father, we thank you for the gift of life, for the breath that sustains life, and for giving us life to continually praise You.

Thank you, Lord, for the help you have given us in the past and the help you will give us again in the future, in Jesus' name.

Deliverance

THE LORD IS A MIGHTY DELIVERER. TIME AND TIME AGAIN, HE HAS SHOWN UP FOR HIS CHILDREN. HE DELIVERED THE ISRAELITES FROM BONDAGE, DELIVERED DANIEL FROM THE LION'S DEN, AND DELIVERED THE THREE HEBREW BOYS FROM THE FIERY FURNACE. HE IS THE SAME YESTERDAY, TODAY AND FOREVER MORE. HE WILL DELIVER YOU AS YOU PRAY.

MANY ARE THE AFFLICTIONS OF THE RIGHTEOUS. BUT THE LORD DELIVERS HIM OUT OF THEM ALL (PSALMS 34:19) AS YOU SEEK THE LORD IN PRAYER, HE WILL HEAR YOU AND DELIVER YOU FROM ALL YOUR FEARS. LET US PRAY!

32. *Psalms 68:19-20* " *What a glorious Lord! He who daily bears our burdens also gives us our salvation. He frees us! He rescues us from death." (TLB).*

Father, I cast my burdens on you. Set me free from the spirit of fear and worry in the name of Jesus. Rescue me from the traps of death laid for me by the evil ones, in the name of Jesus.

33. *Psalms 68:30* *"Rebuke our enemies, O Lord. Bring them– submissive, tax in hand. Scatter all who delight in war." (TLB).*

Father, rebuke our enemies, bring them under our submission and let them pay back seven times what they have stolen from us, in the name of Jesus!

34. *1 Corinthians 14:33 "For God is not the author of confusion, but of peace, as in the churches of all saints." (KJV).*

Lord, we break every cycle of confusion operating in our lives, in our homes, and in our business or workplace, in the name of Jesus!

35. *Isaiah 45:3 "I will give you the treasures of darkness, riches stored in secret places, so that you may know that I am the LORD, the God of Israel, who summons you by name." (NKJV).*

Father, I pray for anyone whose business has been doing well before, but the enemy blew evil wind on it, and the business is in coma. I pray they receive your deliverance in the name of Jesus!

36. *Isaiah 61:7 "Instead of shame and dishonor, you will enjoy a double share of honor. You will possess a double portion of prosperity in your land, and everlasting joy will be yours." (NLT).*

God, arise and fill my mouth with laughter. Let my tears and shame expire, in the name of Jesus!

37. *Joshua 5:9 "Then the Lord said to Joshua, "This day I have rolled away the reproach of Egypt from you." Therefore, the name of the place is called Gilgal to this day." (NKJV).*

Father, today roll away every reproach of my life in the name of Jesus. Turn my tears to cheers in the name of Jesus.

38. *Exodus 12:42 "It is a night to be much observed unto the LORD for bringing them out from the land of Egypt: this is that night of the LORD to be observed of all the children of Israel in their generations". (KJV).*

Father, make tonight "that night of the Lord." Let it be my last day of struggling in life. Humiliate every Pharaoh trying to keep me in bondage in the name of Jesus!

39. *Psalms 105: 1-2 Oh, give thanks to the Lord! Call upon His name; Make known His deeds among the peoples! Sing to Him, sing psalms to Him; Talk of his wondrous works! (NKJV).*

Father, in the name of Jesus, we thank you for your wondrous works among us here at this house of God; For the healings, deliverances, blessings, gifts of life, and so many good things to mention, we Thank You, Lord.

40. *2 Samuel 22: 49-50 "He delivers me from my enemies. You also lift me up above those who rise against me; You have delivered me from the violent man; Therefore, I will give thanks to You, O Lord, among the Gentiles; And sing praises to Your name." (NKJV).*

Father, we thank and give you praise because you delivered our senior pastor and his family, the leadership, and individuals from those who revolted against us, and from violent men. You show mercy to Your anointed and our generations forever. Thank You Lord.

Spiritual Warfare

Spiritual warfare is not a strange thing to believers. Our enemy is satan and his demons. We rejoice because we fight in victory and not for victory. Jesus won the victory for us in Calvary.

"For The weapons of our warfare are not carnal but mighty in God for pulling down strongholds" 2 Corinthians 10:4. It is time to exercise your authority over Satan. Receive your victory. Let us pray!

41. *Psalms 108:13 "Through God we will do valiantly, For it is He who shall tread down our enemies". (NKJV).*

Father, I destroy every power preventing me from enjoying the goodness of The Lord in this land in the name of Jesus! Father, I declare that I will do great exploits in this land!

42. *1 Corinthians 3:11 "For no one is empowered to lay an alternative foundation other than the good foundation that exists, which is Jesus Christ!" (TPT).*

I decree and declare that every alternative foundation against my life is disempowered today, in the mighty name of Jesus! Jesus Christ is the foundation before all other foundations; Therefore, I am rooted in Christ the solid rock in the name of Jesus Christ!

43. *Psalms 144:5, 7-8 "Step down out of heaven, God; ignite volcanoes in the hearts of the mountains...Reach all the way from sky to sea: pull me out of the ocean of hate, out of the grip* *of those barbarians. Who lie through their teeth, who shake your hand then knife you in the back." (Message).*

Father, disgrace all who are incensed against our pastors, all who work in this church, our church and every member of our church. In their presence, make us your voice and establish your presence in our midst, in the name of Jesus!

44. *Psalms 120:6-7 "My soul has dwelt too long with one who hates peace. I am for peace; But when I speak, they are for war." (NKJV).*

Father, we destroy every instrument of war – physical, verbal, or spiritual – raised against our church and church family, and against your servant and his family, in the name of Jesus!

45. *Micah 2:13 "Then I, GOD, will burst all confinements and lead them out into the open. They'll follow their King. I will be out in front leading them." (Message). Micah 2:13 "The One who breaks open the way will go up before them, they will break through the gate and go out. Their King will pass through before them, the LORD at their head." (NIV).*

By the reason of this season, I break out. – My King is JESUS! He passes before me. My Lord is JESUS! He is at my head. I am breaking forth; I am breaking through. I recognize no limit. – The BREAKER is going ahead of me. The Breaker's Anointing is going ahead of me, destroying every obstacle in my path. Mountains before me, obstacles in my way, by the reason of what Christ did, be moved in Jesus' name.

46. Romans 8:32 *"He who did not spare His own Son, but delivered Him up for us all, how shall He not with Him also freely give us all things?" (NKJV).*

Romans 8:31-32 "So, what do you think? With God on our side like this, how can we lose? If God didn't hesitate to put everything on the line for us, embracing our condition and exposing himself to the worst by sending his own Son, is there anything else he wouldn't gladly and freely do for us?" (Message).

Lord, I declare that every spiritual castration in my life is reversed.

47. *Romans 8:11 "But if the Spirit of Him who raised Jesus from the dead dwells in you, He who raised Christ from the dead will also give life to your mortal bodies through His Spirit, who dwells in you." (NKJV).*

Every deadness in my life, I command you to be quickened by the Spirit of God.

48. *Ezekiel 18: 20 "The soul who sins shall die. The son shall not bear the guilt of the father, nor the father bear the guilt of the son. The righteousness of the righteous shall be upon himself, and the wickedness of the wicked shall be upon himself." (NKJV).*

Father in your compassion and mercy, we come against any, and all generational curses that the enemy tries to unleash on any member of this church. We claim the blessings in the work of God that the teeth of your children at this church will never be set on edge because of the errors or mistakes of their forebears in Jesus' name.

49. *Colossians 2:14-15 "having wiped out the handwriting of requirements that was against us, which was contrary to us. And He has taken it out of the way, having nailed it to the cross. 15. Having disarmed principalities and powers, He made a public spectacle of them, triumphing over them in it." (NKJV).*

Whatever cannot hold Christ, will not hold me down.

50. *Acts 2: 46-47 "So continuing daily with one accord in the temple, and breaking bread from house to house, they ate their food with gladness and simplicity of heart, praising God and having favor with all the people. And the Lord added to the church daily those who were being saved. (NKJV).*

Father in the name of Jesus, we declare that as we worship and praise you in this house and break bread, the spirit of revival will rest upon us that will breakout into the community, and Nation at large. We will go from house to house preaching the gospel and having favor with the people. Souls will be added to Your kingdom in Jesus Name.

51. *Isaiah 33:20 "Look upon Zion, the city of our appointed feasts; Your eyes will see Jerusalem, a quiet home, a tabernacle that will not be taken down; not one of its stakes will ever be removed, nor will any of its cords be broken." (NKJV).*

Father, frustrate and cast down every power planning to wage war against the divine vision of our church, every member of our church and his family, in the name of Jesus!

52. *Exodus 4:19 "Now the Lord said to Moses in Midian, "Go, return to Egypt, for all the men who sought your life are dead." (NKJV).*

Father, paralyze anyone or group of people planning to destroy my destiny in the name of Jesus.

53. *Psalms 2:8 "Ask of Me, and I will surely give the [a]nations as Your inheritance, And the very ends of the earth as Your possession." (NASB).*

Father, we ask that in this year, the Gospel of our Lord Jesus Christ will flourish and reign mightily across the nations of the earth. That many more nations will open their borders to Missionaries and to the Gospel of Christ. In such nations, violence shall cease, and peace shall reign!

54. *Isaiah 50:7 "For the Lord God will help Me; Therefore, I will not be disgraced; Therefore I have set My face like a flint, And I know that I will not be ashamed. (NKJV).*

Father, I bind every spirit of frustration, defeat, delayed blessing, and fear in my environment, in the name of Jesus!

55. *Ecclesiastes 10:7; "I have seen servants on horses, while princes walk on the ground like servants." (NKJV).*

Father, I destroy every vulture released by the enemy to eat or hinder my destiny and that of my family, in the name of Jesus!

56. *Psalms 68:30 "Rebuke our enemies, O Lord. Bring them— submissive, tax in hand. Scatter all who delight in war." (TLB).*

Father, rebuke my enemies, let them submit themselves to me and make me rulers over those who hate me in the name of Jesus.

57. *Matthew 14:24 "But the ship was now in the midst of the sea, tossed with waves: for the wind was contrary." (KJV).*

We stop every contrary wind against our church, every member of our church, and your servant and his family, in the name of Jesus!

58. *Matthew 9:37-38 "Then He said to His disciples "The harvest is truly plentiful, but the laborers are few. Therefore, pray the Lord of the harvest to send out laborers into His harvest." (NKJV).*

Father, open our eyes to the harvest before us. Lead us as a church to go out in the fields and get to work. We thank you that you will raise up men, women, and children to make disciples here and around the world.

59. *Job 5:12 "He frustrates the devices of the crafty, so that their hands cannot carry out their plans." (NKJV).*

Lord, build a wall of protection around our pastor, his wife, and their children, in the name of Jesus. Let every plan against them be frustrated, in the name of Jesus.

60. *Psalms 37:23-24; "The Lord directs the steps of the godly. He delights in every detail of their lives. Though they stumble, they will never fall, for the Lord holds them by the hand." (NLT).*

Father, I pray against every false open door (pseudo-blessing) that could lead to physical or spiritual destruction of our church members and its leadership, in the name of Jesus!

61. Psalms 68:1-2 *"God is already beginning to arise, and His enemies to scatter; let them also who hate Him flee before Him! As smoke is driven away, so drive them away; as wax melts before the fire, so let the wicked perish before the presence of God."* (Amplified).

Arise O God and scatter all the enemies of our church and let those who plan evil against our church and its members be put to shame.

62. 2 Corinthians 10:5 *"Casting down imaginations, and every high thing that exalteth itself against the knowledge of God..." (KJV).*

I pray that every attack and evil imagination against our church, its leadership and membership are stopped, cast down and destroyed, in the name of Jesus!

63. 2 Chronicles 14:3 *"For he removed that altar of foreign gods and the high places and broke down the sacred pillars and cut down the wooden images." (NKJV).*

I pray we destroy every strange and foreign altar raised against our church, every member of our church and your servant and his family, in the name of Jesus!

64. Isaiah 37:14 *"Then Hezekiah took the letter from the hand of the messengers and read it, and he went up to the house of the LORD and spread it out before the LORD. (NIV).*

Father, I declare that every letter, email, or text written against me and concerning my destiny, becomes my instrument of testimony, in the name of Jesus!

65. *Psalms 23:5 "You prepare a table before me in the presence of my enemies; You anoint my head with oil; My cup runs over." (NKJV).*

Father, those who say I will not reach my goal, vision, or destiny, paralyze them so that when I reach my goal, vision, or destiny, they will be able to see Your glory over me, in the name of Jesus!

66. *Psalms 7:6 "Arise, O Lord, in Your anger; Lift Yourself up because of the rage of my enemies; Rise up for me to the judgment You have commanded! (NKJV).*

Every rage of the enemy against my destiny, scatter in the name of Jesus!

67. *Psalms 37:14-15 "The wicked draw the sword and bend the bow to bring down the poor and needy, to slay those whose ways are upright. 15 But their swords will pierce their own hearts, and their bows will be broken." (NIV).*

Owner of evil load, I command you to carry your load in the name of Jesus!

68. *Jeremiah 31:29 "In those days they shall say no more: "The Fathers have eaten sour grapes, and the children's teeth are set on edge."(NKJV).*

Father, I declare that from today, the failure that happened in the lives of my parents will not happen in my life and in the lives of my children, in the name of Jesus!

69. *Psalms 3:7 "Up, God! My God, help me! Slap their faces, first this cheek, then the other, Your fist hard in their teeth!" (Message).*

Father, I command my guardian angels to slap all unprofitable and evil broadcasters of my goodness, and of our church and of our pastors; and silence them in the name of Jesus!

70. *Ezekiel 34:5 "And now they're scattered every which way because there was no shepherd—scattered and easy pickings for wolves and coyotes." (Message).*

Father, I destroy every organized network of demonic wickedness against our Shepherds and Pastors, and their family; and frustrate every negative utterance declared against them in the name of Jesus!

71. *Isaiah 49:26 "And your enemies, crazed and desperate, will turn on themselves, killing each other in a frenzy of self-destruction. Then everyone will know that I, God, have saved you—I, the Mighty One of Jacob." (Message).*

Father, I declare, any power planning untimely death for me this year, die in my place, in the name of Jesus!

72. *Hebrews 6:3 "And so, God willing, we will move forward to further understanding." (NLT).*

Father, I break myself loose from the bondage of life stagnation. I shall move forward and reverse every evil arrangement setup for my life, in the name of Jesus!

73. *Numbers 23:23 "For there is no sorcery against Jacob, nor any divination against Israel. It must be said of Jacob and of Israel, "Oh, what God has done!" (NKJV).*

Father, let every spell, jinx, and demonic incantation rendered against every member of our church be canceled, in the name of Jesus.

74. *Numbers 23:5 "Nevertheless the Lord your God would not listen to Balaam, but the Lord your God turned the curse into a blessing for you, because the Lord your God loves you. (NKJV).*

Father, I declare that every curse pronounced against our church, our pastors and every member of our church, turns into a blessing for us, in the name of Jesus! Disgrace every Balaam raised against us in the name of Jesus!

75. *Psalms 3:7 "Up, God! My God, help me! Slap their faces, first this cheek, then the other, Your fist hard in their teeth!" (Message).*

Father, I command my guardian angels to slap all unprofitable and evil broadcasters of my goodness, our church and our pastors, and silence them in the name of Jesus!

76. *Isaiah 49:26 "And your enemies, crazed and desperate, will turn on themselves, killing each other in a frenzy of self-destruction.*

Then everyone will know that I, God, have save Mighty One of Jacob." (Message).

Father, I declare, any power planning untimely death for me this year, die in my place, in the name of Jesus!

77. *Hebrews 6:3 "And so, God willing, we will move forward to further understanding." (NLT).*

Father, I break myself loose from the bondage of life stagnation. I shall move forward and reverse every evil arrangement setup for my life, in the name of Jesus!

78. *Isaiah 49:26 "And your enemies, crazed and desperate, will turn on themselves, killing each other in a frenzy of self-destruction. Then everyone will know that I, God, have saved you—I, the Mighty One of Jacob." (Message).*

Father, we send confusion into the camp of any group ganging up against our pastors, and against our church. Let them turn on each other in a frenzy of self-destruction, in the name of Jesus!

79. *Jeremiah 1:19 "They will fight against you, but they shall not prevail against you. For I am with you, says the LORD, to deliver you." (NKJV).*

Father, we declare that every attack against our pastors and their children shall not prevail in the name of Jesus! We receive victory for our pastors; grant them peace on every side in the name of Jesus!

80. *Jeremiah 31:29 "In those days they shall say no more: "The Fathers have eaten sour grapes, and the children's teeth are set on edge." (NKJV).*

Father, I declare that from today, the failure that happened in the lives of my parents, will not happen in my life or in the lives of my children, in the name of Jesus!

81. *Psalms 16:1-2 Preserve me, O God, for in You I put my trust. O my soul, you have said to the Lord, "You are my Lord, my goodness is nothing apart from You." (NKJV).*

Father, frustrate every territorial spirit working against our church, pastors, and members of our church, in the name of Jesus!

82. *Zephaniah 3:15 "The LORD has taken away your judgements, He has cast out your enemy. The King of Israel, The LORD, is in your midst; you shall see disaster no more." (NKJV).*

Father, take away from our church any judgment against us, cast away all our enemies as you have promised. Rule in our midst throughout this year and let us see no disaster in the name of Jesus!

83. *Isaiah 17:14 "Then behold, at eventide, trouble! And before the morning, he is no more. This is the portion of those who plunder us, and the lot of those who rob us." (NKJV).*

Father, frustrate and disgrace anyone that threatens to plunder or rob our pastors of relevance and impact; home and abroad, in the name of Jesus!

84. Luke 8:17 *"For nothing is secret that will not be revealed, nor anything hidden that will not be known and come to light."* (NKJV).

Lord, bring to light and expose everything planned in darkness, against our church, its members, and our pastor's family, in the name of Jesus!

85. Judges 8:28 *"That is the story of how the people of Israel defeated Midian, which never recovered. Throughout the rest of Gideon's lifetime–about forty years–there was peace in the land."* (NLT).

Father, defeat and scatter all those who plot to see me fail and do not let them recover again, in the name of Jesus. Surround me all around with your peace.

86. Psalms 44:4-5 *"You're my King, O God—command victories for Jacob! With your help we'll wipe out our enemies, in your name we'll stomp them to dust."* (Message).

Father, we destroy and wipe out every attack and gang-up against our church, its members, and our pastors. We receive our victory in the name of Jesus!

87. Isaiah 50:11 *"But if all you're after is making trouble, playing with fire, go ahead and see where it gets you. Set your fires, stir people up, blow on the flames, but don't expect me to just stand there and watch. I'll hold your feet to those flames."* (Message).

Father, frustrate and destroy anything or anyone planning against our pastors, and their family. Hold the feet of the wicked to the flames of fire that they set up for our pastors, in the name of Jesus!

88. *1 Corinthians 2:12 – Now we have received, not the spirit of the world, but the Spirit who is from God, that we might know the things that have been freely given to us by God. (NKJV).*

Father, everything that belongs to me that the enemy is trying to hide from me, restore them to me, in the name of Jesus. Lord let me begin to enjoy everything that you have freely given to me, (health, wealth, prosperity) in the name of Jesus!

89. *Isaiah 33:20 "Look upon Zion, the city of our appointed feasts; Your eyes will see Jerusalem, a quiet home, a Tabernacle that will not be taken down; not one of its stakes will ever be removed, nor will any of its cords be broken." (NKJV).*

Father, frustrate and cast down every power planning to wage war against the divine vision of our church, our pastors, and every member of our church, in the name of Jesus!

90. *Job 5:12 "He frustrates the devices of the crafty, so that their hands cannot carry out their plans." (NKJV).*

Lord, build a wall of protection around our pastors and their children, in the name of Jesus. Let every plan against them be frustrated, in the name of Jesus!

91. *Judges 8:28 "That is the story of how the people of Israel defeated Midian, which never recovered. Throughout the rest of Gideon's lifetime–about forty years–there was peace in the land." (NLT).*

Father, defeat and scatter all those who are plotting to see me fail, and do not let them recover again, in the name of Jesus. Surround me all around with your peace.

92. *Psalms 44:4-5 "You're my King, O God—command victories for Jacob! With your help we'll wipe out our enemies, in your name we'll stomp them to dust." (Message).*

Father, we destroy and wipe out every attack and gang-up against our church, its members and our pastors. We receive our victory in the name of Jesus!

93. *Psalms 18:24 "God rewrote the text of my life when I opened the book of my heart to his eyes." (Message).*

Father, rewrite the text of my life, fill in the details of your blessings and cancel every agenda of the wicked against me, my family, and our church, in the name of Jesus!

94. *Joshua 5:9 "Then the Lord said to Joshua, "This day I have rolled away the reproach of Egypt from you." Therefore, the name of the place is called Gilgal to this day." (NKJV).*

Father, I declare that every pain and struggle of the past year will not follow me into this new year. Roll away every reproach of my life, in the name of Jesus. In this new year, turn my tears to cheers, in the name of Jesus.

95. *Psalms 16: 9-10 "I'm happy from the inside out, and from the outside in, I'm firmly formed. You canceled my ticket to hell— that's not my destination!" (Message).*

Father, I cancel today every grave dug for any member of our church in this new year. I declare that no one will die in our midst, in the name of Jesus!

96. *Judges 8:28 "That is the story of how the people of Israel defeated Midian, which never recovered. Throughout the rest of Gideon's lifetime–about forty years–there was peace in the land." (NLT).*

Father, defeat and scatter all those who are plotting to see me fail and do not let them recover again, in the name of Jesus. Surround me all around with your peace.

97. *Psalms 44:4-5 "You're my King, O God—command victories for Jacob! With your help we'll wipe out our enemies, in your name we'll stomp them to dust." (Message).*

Father, we destroy and wipe out every attack and gang-up against our church, our members, and our pastors. We receive our victory, in the name of Jesus!

98. *Psalms 3:7 "Up, God! My God, help me! Slap their faces, first this cheek, then the other, Your fist hard in their teeth!" (Message).*

Father, I command my guardian angels to slap all unprofitable and evil broadcasters of my goodness and of our church and pastors, and silence them, in the name of Jesus!

99. *Ezekiel 34:5 "And now they're scattered every which way because there was no shepherd—scattered and easy pickings for wolves and coyotes."(Message).*

Father, I destroy every organized network of demonic wickedness against our Shepherds and Pastors, and their family; and frustrate every negative utterance declared against them, in the name of Jesus!

100. Isaiah 49:26 *"And your enemies, crazed and desperate, will turn on themselves, killing each other in a frenzy of self-destruction. Then everyone will know that I, God, have saved you—I, the Mighty One of Jacob." (Message).*

Father, I declare, any power planning untimely death for me this year, die in my place, in the name of Jesus!

101. Hebrews 6:3 *"And so, God willing, we will move forward to further understanding."(NLT).*

Father, I break myself loose from the bondage of life stagnation. I shall move forward and reverse every evil arrangement setup for my life, in the name of Jesus!

102. Matthew 14:24 *"But the ship was now in the midst of the sea, tossed with waves: for the wind was contrary." (KJV).*

We stop every contrary wind against our church, our pastor's family and every member of our church in the name of Jesus!

103. Psalms 68:28 *"Your God has commanded your strength, strengthen, O God, what You have done for us." (NKJV).*

O Lord, let no man prevail against our church, its leadership, and membership, in the name of Jesus!

104. Psalms 44:4-5 *"You're my King, O God—command victories for Jacob! With your help we'll wipe out our enemies, in your name we'll stomp them to dust." (Message).*

Father, we destroy and wipe out every attack and gang-up against our church, its members, and our pastors. We receive our victory, in the name of Jesus!

105. Matthew 10:1 *"And when He had called His twelve disciples to Him, He gave them power over unclean spirits, to cast them out, and to heal all kinds of sickness and all kinds of disease." (NKJV).*

Lord, release fresh unction unto our church as a ministry, and use this church to destroy the satanic kingdom in this nation and all over the world, in the name of Jesus.

106. Esther 7:10 *"So they hanged Haman on the gallows that he had prepared for Mordecai. Then the king's wrath subsided. (NKJV).*

Father, let my enemies be hanged on the pole they had set up for me. Let them be hanged on the gallows which they had prepared for me.

107. Psalms 18:36 *"You cleared the ground under me, so my footing was firm. (Message).*

Father, hold me firmly and let nothing pull me down. Set my footing firmly on your word and make me an example of the power of your word in the name of Jesus.

108. Jeremiah 30:19 *"Then out of them shall proceed thanksgiving and the voice of those who make merry; I will multiply them, and they shall not diminish; I will also glorify them, and they shall not be small. (NKJV).*

Father, we destroy and pull down every form of limitation structured against our church in the name of Jesus Christ.

109. Matthew 9:38 *"Therefore pray The Lord of the harvest to send out laborers into His harvest." (NKJV).*

Lord, bring the workers of Your choice to our church and keep all other evil agents away, in the name of Jesus!

110. Numbers 23:23 *"No curse can touch Jacob; no magic has any power against Israel. For now, it will be said of Jacob, 'What wonders God has done for Israel!" (NLT).*

Father, we destroy every instrument of war (physical, verbal, or spiritual) raised against our pastors and their family, in the name of Jesus. Disgrace and humiliate those who want them to fail in the name of Jesus.

111. Isaiah 55:13 *"No more thistles, but giant sequoias, no more thornbushes, but stately pines— Monuments to me, to God, living and lasting evidence of God." (Message).*

Father, every root curse of poverty and inability to multiply resources, I command it to leave my life alone, in the mighty name of Jesus Christ!

112. *Galatians 5:10 "...The one who is throwing you into confusion will pay the penalty, whoever he may be. (NIV).*

Father, in the mighty name of Jesus Christ, I break all satanic and wicked powers that keep me moving in a circle without any tangible result or achievement.

113. *Isaiah 17:14 "At bedtime, terror fills the air. By morning it's gone—not a sign of it anywhere! This is what happens to those who would ruin us, this is the fate of those out to get us." (Message).*

Father, frustrate and disgrace anyone that threatens to plunder or rob our pastors of relevance and impact, home and abroad, in the name of Jesus!

114. *Deuteronomy 1:6-7 "Back at Horeb, God, our God, spoke to us: "You've stayed long enough at this mountain. On your way now. Get moving." (Message).*

Father, in the precious name of Jesus Christ, I command every embargo of stagnation and limitation on my life to break and shatter to pieces now!

115. *2 Timothy 1:7 "For God has not given us a spirit of fear, but of power and of love and of a sound mind." (NKJV).*

Father, because you have not given me the spirit of fear but of love, power, and of a sound mind, I hereby arrest the spirit of fear, anxiety, depression and cast them out of my life, in Jesus mighty name I pray!

116. *Exodus 4:17 "And you shall take this rod in your hand, with which you shall do the signs." (NKJV).*

Father, I hold the rod of God in my hands. I smash the head of every oppressor in the name of Jesus!

117. *1 Samuel 17:54 "And David took the head of the Philistine and brought it to Jerusalem, but he put his armor in his tent." (NKJV).*

O God, arise and place the head of my Goliath in my hands, in the name of Jesus!

118. *1 Samuel 30: 4 & 17 "Then David and the people who were with him lifted their voices and wept, until they had no more power to weep... Then David attacked them from twilight until the evening of the next day. Not a man of them escaped, except four hundred young men who rode on camels and fled." (NKJV).*

Father, crush and destroy the power that has made me cry in the name of Jesus!

119. *1 Samuel 17:49 "Then David put his hand in his bag and took out a stone; and he slung it and struck the Philistine in his forehead, so that the stone sank into his forehead, and he fell on his face to the earth." (NKJV).*

Father, let my stone locate the forehead of my Goliath and smash it, in the name of Jesus!

120. Isaiah 54:15 *"Behold they shall surely gather together, but not by me: whosoever shall gather together against thee shall fall for thy sake." (KJV).*

Father, scatter all those who gathered to celebrate my fall and clothe them with shame in the name of Jesus!

121. Acts 23:21 *"More than forty men are hiding and waiting to kill Paul. They have all taken an oath not to eat or drink until they have killed him. Now they are waiting for you to agree." (NCV).*

Father, we annul, revoke, and renounce every evil vow, every evil association, evil network, and evil alliance against the advancement of our church and of our pastors, in the name of Jesus.

122. Proverbs 4:18 *"The ways of right-living people glow with light; the longer they live, the brighter they shine." (Message).*

Father, in this year, no area of our lives will experience darkness, we shall live brighter, and we shall shine brighter in all areas of our lives, in the name of Jesus.

123. Isaiah 54:17 *"Weapons made to attack you won't be successful; words spoken against you won't hurt at all. My servant, Jerusalem is yours! I, the Lord, promise to bless you with victory." (CEV).*

Every weapon (physical, verbal, or spiritual) that is made to attack our pastors and their children, won't be successful. Every wicked gossiper and evil broadcaster of our pastors and his family will suffer shame and devastations in the name of Jesus!

124. Psalms 68:30 *"Rebuke our enemies, O Lord. Bring them–submissive, tax in hand. Scatter all who delight in war." (TLB).*

Father, rebuke all the enemies of our pastors, and their family. Let their enemies submit themselves to them and make our pastors rulers over those who hate him, in the name of Jesus.

125. *Psalms 121:7-8 "The Lord keeps you from all harm and watches over your life. The Lord keeps watch over you as you come and go, both now and forever. (NLT).*

Father, we declare that no one in our church family will die this year. No one shall be missing nor suffer loss, in the name of Jesus.

126. *2 Chronicles 29:36 "And Hezekiah and all the people rejoiced because of what God had done for the people, for everything had been accomplished so quickly." (NLT).*

Father, we declare no more delay and no more slowdown, in the name of Jesus. Everything will work out quickly for us this year in the name of Jesus.

127. *Esther 7:10 "So Haman was hanged on the very gallows that he had built for Mordecai. And the king's hot anger cooled." (Message).*

Father, let my enemies be hanged on the pole they had set up for me. Let them be hanged on the gallows which they had prepared for me.

128. *Numbers 16:48 "And he took his place between the dead and the living: and the disease was stopped." (BBE).*

Father, we declare that we take our place as the royal priesthood that God has made us, and we stop the plague of any pandemic in the name of Jesus!

129. *Job 38:11 "I said, 'This far and no farther will you come. Here your proud waves must stop!'" (NLT).*

Father, we decree and declare that any pandemic and any disease thus far, you will come. Your proud waves stop now. You will go no farther, in the name of Jesus!

130. *Numbers 16:48 "And he took his place between the dead and the living: and the disease was stopped." (BBE).*

We take our place as the royal priesthood that God has made us, and we stop the plague of any pandemic, in the name of Jesus!

131. *Jeremiah 16:16-17 "But now I am sending for many fishermen who will catch them," says the LORD. "I am sending for hunters who will hunt them down in the mountains, hills, and caves. I am watching them closely, and I see every sin. They cannot hope to hide from me." (NLT).*

Father, arise and hunt down all those who are playing politics with the lives of the people of all over the world. Fish and flush them out, in the name of Jesus. Expose their wickedness and let them have no place to hide again, in the name of Jesus.

132. Psalms 24:9 *"So wake up, you living gateways, and rejoice! Fling wide, you ageless doors of destiny! Here he comes; the King of Glory is ready to come in." (Passion).*

Father, we declare every closed door of opportunities, of promotion, of success, of increase, of favor, and of honor begin to open for me now, in the name of Jesus. Lead the way and cause every closed door to open, in the name of Jesus.

133. Psalms 69:29-30 *"But rescue me, O God, from my poverty and pain. Then I will praise God with my singing! My thanks will be his praise. (TLB).*

Father, rescue me from poverty and pain. Let favor locate me and terminate labor and toiling in my life, in the name of Jesus.

134. Psalms 108:13 *"With God's help we will prevail with might and power. And with God's help we'll trample down our every foe!" (Passion).*

Father, I destroy every power preventing me from enjoying the goodness of The Lord in this land, in the name of Jesus!

135. Isaiah 54:17 *"Weapons made to attack you won't be successful; words spoken against you won't hurt at all. My servant, Jerusalem is yours! I, the Lord, promise to bless you with victory." (CEV).*

Every weapon (physical, verbal, or spiritual) made to attack our pastors and their children, won't be successful. Every wicked gossiper and evil broadcasters of our pastors and their families will suffer shame and devastations, in the name of Jesus!

136. *Psalms 68:30 "Rebuke our enemies, O Lord. Bring them–submissive, tax in hand. Scatter all who delight in war." (TLB).*

Father, rebuke all the enemies of our pastors and their families. Let their enemies submit themselves, and make our pastors ruler over those who hate them, in the name of Jesus.

137. *Job 5:12 "He aborts the schemes of conniving crooks, so that none of their plots come to term." (Message).*

Father, we abort and nullify every scheme of conniving crooks against every member of our church family, in the name of Jesus. No one in our church will suffer defeat this year, in the name of Jesus.

138. *Isaiah 50:7 "But if all you're after is making trouble, playing with fire, Go ahead and see where it gets you. Set your fires, stir people up, blow on the flames, But don't expect me to just stand there and watch. I'll hold your feet to those flames. (Message).*

Father, hold the feet of those who plan to hurt our church and members, to fire and let them burn in the flames that they set for us, in the name of Jesus.

139. *Psalms 121:7-8 "The Lord keeps you from all harm and watches over your life. 8 The Lord keeps watch over you as you come and go, both now and forever. (NLT).*

Father, we declare that no one in our church family will die this year. No one shall be missing, no one will suffer loss, in the name of Jesus.

140. *2 Chronicles 29:36 "And Hezekiah and all the people rejoiced because of what God had done for the people, for everything had been accomplished so quickly." (NLT).*

Father, we declare no more delay and no more slow-down in the name of Jesus. Everything will work out quickly for us this year, in the name of Jesus.

141. *Isaiah 26:6 "The time will come when Israel will take root and bud and blossom and fill the whole earth with her fruit!" (TLB).*

Father, the time has come to establish your son, our pastor, as your voice to the nations. Let him take root in every continent of the world, and bud and blossom, in the name of Jesus. Justify your anointing upon his life through miracles, signs, and wonders in the name of Jesus.

142. *2 Chronicles 14:7 "…we have this peaceful land because we sought GOD; he has given us rest from all troubles." So they built and enjoyed prosperity." (Message).*

Father, we declare peace and prosperity upon everyone that has given, and continues to give, to the ministries of our church. Let their hands always remain on top, and let none of them suffer loss, in the name of Jesus!

143. *Esther 2:21-22 "Now Bigthana and Teresh were two of the king's eunuchs who guarded the doorway. While Mordecai was sitting at the king's gate, they became angry and began to make plans to kill King Xerxes. 22 But Mordecai found out about their plans and told Queen Esther. Then Esther told the king how Mordecai had discovered the evil plan." (NCV).*

Father, expose every evil plan and imagination against our pastors and their children. Let every Bigthana and Teresh hang themselves, in the name of Jesus.

144. *John 9:5 "As long as I am with you my life is the light that pierces the world's darkness." (TPT).*

Father, let your light pierce every darkness in my life, home, finances, health, business, and family, in the name of Jesus. Shine your light on me and make me a success story in this nation, in the name of Jesus.

145. *Psalms 29:11 "This is the one who gives his strength and might to his people. This is the Lord giving us his kiss of peace." (TPT).*

Father, give me Your kiss of peace in every area of my life, in the name of Jesus. As we come to the end of this year, let your peace surround me.

146. *Psalms 30:11 "Then he broke through and transformed all my wailing into a whirling dance of ecstatic praise He has torn the veil and lifted from me the sad heaviness of mourning. He wrapped me in the glory garments of gladness." (TPT).*

Father, breakthrough for me and transform my tears and pain into a dance of ecstatic praise. Tear from me any garment capable of producing mourning or heaviness of the heart, and wrap me with glorious garments of joy and gladness, in the name of Jesus.

147. Psalms 119:31 *"Lord, don't allow me to make a mess of my life, for I cling to your commands and follow them as closely as I can." (TPT).*

Father, don't let me make a mess of my life, give me discernment to discover every trap the enemy has laid for me and to avoid them.

148. *Psalms 119:66 "Teach me how to make good decisions, and give me revelation-light, for I believe in your commands." (TPT).*

Father, teach me how to make good decisions and do not let me go astray, in the name of Jesus. Guide my steps and order my life to glorify You, in the name of Jesus.

149. *Psalms 31:16 "Smile on me, your servant. Let your undying love and glorious grace save me from all this gloom." (TPT).*

Father, continue to smile on our pastors and their children, in the name of Jesus. Let your undying love and glorious grace surround them continually and protect them from all haters, in the name of Jesus.

150. *Psalms 31:20 "So hide all your beloved ones in the sheltered, secret place before your face. Overshadow them by your glory-*

presence. Keep them from these accusations, the brutal insults of evil men. Tuck them safely away in the tabernacle where you dwell." (TPT).

Father, hide our pastors and their children in the secret place before your face. Let the glory of your presence overshadow them continually, in the name of Jesus. Keep them insulated and protected from accusations and insults of wicked and evil people, in the name of Jesus.

151. *Galatians 1:17 "And I chose not to run to Jerusalem to try to impress those who had become apostles before me. Instead, I went away into the Arabian Desert for a season until I returned to Damascus, where I had first encountered Jesus." (TPT).*

Father, deliver me from my sin of pleasing people. Lead me back to the place I had first encountered, Jesus. Lead me back to my first love and let the fire of the Holy Spirit burn brightly inside me and through me, in the name of Jesus.

152. *Galatians 1:24 "Because of the transformation that took place in my life, they praised God even more!" (TPT).*

Father, let the testimonies of your hand upon our church cause many to praise you even more, in the name of Jesus. Transform our lives continually so that we will always point people to your saving grace, in the name of Jesus. Let us bear fruit that will remain forever, in the name of Jesus.

153. *Psalms 28: 5 "Since they don't care anything about you, or about the great things you've done, take them down like an old building being demolished, never again to be rebuilt." (TPT).*

Father, take them down like old buildings being demolished. Take down all those who attacked, or plan to attack our church, our vision, our leadership, and membership. Never let our haters rise again in the name of Jesus.

154. 1 Kings 3:3 *"Solomon loved GOD and continued to live in the God-honoring ways of David his father, except that he also worshiped at the local shrines, offering sacrifices and burning incense." (Message).*

Father, show me every local shrine in my life, and give me the courage to destroy them. Help me to live a life that pleases you, in the name of Jesus.

155. Hebrews 10:24 *"Discover creative ways to encourage others and to motivate them toward acts of compassion, doing beautiful works as expressions of love." (PASSION).*

Father, make me a blessing to nations. Make me a destiny helper and a lifter of the fallen. I declare that I will impact the lives of many, and nations will come to the brightness of my shining, in the name of Jesus.

156. Exodus 1:7 *"But the children of Israel were fruitful and increased abundantly, multiplied and grew exceedingly mighty; and the land was filled with them." (NKJV).*

Father, we declare that we shall continue to be fruitful and increase abundantly in this land. We shall become exceedingly mighty and powerful. We shall possess the gates of the cities, and make your glories known, in the name of Jesus.

157. *Psalms 119:39 "Defend me from the criticism I face for keeping your beautiful words." (TPT).*

Father, defend and protect our pastors and their children from criticism and careless talk of haters. In the presence of their haters, make them your voice, in the name of Jesus.

158. *Isaiah 54:15 "Behold, they may gather together and stir up strife, but it is not from Me. Whoever stirs up strife against you shall fall and surrender to you." (AMPC).*

Father, we declare that anyone gathering to stir up strife against our pastors and their children, shall fall and never rise again, in the name of Jesus. They shall go down in defeat and will never rise to prominence, in the name of Jesus.

159. *Zechariah 3:2 "And the LORD said to Satan, "The LORD rebuke you, Satan! The LORD who has chosen Jerusalem rebuke you! Is this not a brand plucked from the fire?" (NKJV).*

Satan, the Lord of Host rebukes you over every city in the world, in the mighty name of Jesus! You will not prosper in this land again, in the mighty name of Jesus Christ. We declare peace over our cities, in the name of Jesus.

160. *Proverbs 3:5-6 "Trust in the LORD with all your heart and lean not on your own understanding; 6 In all your ways acknowledge Him, And He shall direct your paths. (NKJV).*

Lord, we declare that all government leaders will fear the Lord and listen carefully to His voice, and that every decision they make would be based on God's will and plan for our countries in this world.

161. *Proverbs 29:2 "When the righteous are in authority, the people rejoice; But when a wicked man rules, the people groan." (NKJV).*

Father, we pray that you will put righteous people in authority in every seat of government all over the world. Direct our heart to vote for those who will promote righteousness and not hate, bigotry or division, in the name of Jesus!

162. *Psalms 2:10-11 "Therefore, you kings, be wise; be warned, you rulers of the earth. Serve the LORD with fear and celebrate his rule with trembling. (NIV).*

Father, we pray for every president and their respective governments. That they will receive wisdom and lead their nations in the fear of God and in the beauty of holiness and love.

163. *Psalms 33:12 "Blessed and prosperous is that nation who has God as their Lord! They will be the people he has chosen for his own." (TPT).*

Father, we declare you as God and Lord over every nation of the world. Bless and prosper every nation again and again. Let your face shine continuously over every nation. No nation shall go down, in the mighty name of Jesus!

164. *Job 14:4 "Who can make a clean thing out of the unclean? No one!" (Amplified).*

Father, you are the only one that can cleanse the unclean. Do it again in every country and continent. Arise Oh Lord, hunt down all those playing politics with the lives of the people of this land, and expose their wickedness. Revive this world again and bless this land.

165. *Psalms 69:23 "Let their eyes be darkened, so that they do not see; And make their loins shake continually. 24. Pour out Your Indignation upon them, And let Your wrathful anger take hold of them." (NKJV).*

Father, darken the eyes of my enemies of progress, make them shake continually and lift me up above their evil thoughts, in the mighty name of Jesus! Pour out your indignation upon them Lord, and let your wrathful anger take hold of them, in the mighty name of Jesus!

166. *Proverbs 4:18 "But the path of the just is as the shining light, that shineth more and more unto the perfect day." (KJV).*

Father, we decree that the vision and mission of this church will go stronger and brighter with greater impact; from one generation to another, in the name of Jesus Christ.

167. *Ephesians 6:19 "And pray for me, too. Ask God to give me the right words so I can boldly explain God's mysterious plan that the Good News is for Jews and Gentiles alike." (NLT).*

Father, by your Spirit, empower all our ministries in this church to deliver their functions with greater effectiveness for the glory of your holy name, and for the blessing of the people here at this church. Grant greater insight unto all ministry leaders to obtain greater results, in the name of Jesus.

168. *Acts 26:16-18 "But rise, and stand upon thy feet: for I have appeared unto thee for this purpose, to make thee a minister and a witness both of these things which thou hast seen, and of those things in the which I will appear unto thee; Delivering thee from the people, and from the Gentiles, unto whom now I send thee, To open their eyes, and to turn them from darkness to light, and from the power of Satan unto God, that they may receive forgiveness of sins, and inheritance among them which are sanctified by faith that is in me." (KJV).*

Father, I am the Light created to bring light to this dark world. Lord, Jesus, don't let my light become darkness. Don't let my light run out. Don't let my light burn out.

169. *Matthew 5:14-16 "Ye are the light of the world. A city that is set on a hill cannot be hid. Neither do men light a candle, and put it under a bushel, but on a candlestick; and it giveth light unto all that are in the house. Let your light so shine before men, that they may see your good works, and glorify your Father which is in heaven." (KJV).*

Father, I am the solution to problems. Don't let me become the problem the world is solving. Increase my capacity to solve problems, in the name of Jesus Christ.

170. *Romans 15:18-19 "For I will not dare to speak of any of those things which Christ hath not wrought by me, to make the Gentiles obedient, by word and deed, Through mighty signs and* *wonders, by the power of the Spirit of God; so that from Jerusalem, and round about unto Illyricum, I have fully preached the gospel of Christ." (KJV).*

Father, in the name of Jesus, let the power of the Holy Ghost turn things around for my good, through mighty signs and wonders. Let the Person, Power and Principles of Christ be fully formed in me!

171. *2 Thessalonians 1:3 "Dear brothers and sisters, we can't help but thank God for you, because your faith is flourishing and your love for one another is growing." (NLT).*

Father, let our children in this church continue to grow in the knowledge, the fear, and power of God continually.

172. *Zechariah 2:3-5 "And there was the angel who talked with me, going out; and another angel was coming out to meet him, who said to him, "Run, speak to this young man, saying: 'Jerusalem shall be inhabited as towns without walls, because of the multitude of men and livestock in it. For I,' says the Lord, 'will be a wall of fire all around her, and I will be the glory in her midst." (NKJV).*

Father, increase this church numerically. Let multitudes of men and women flow into this Church and be established for life by the power of your Word.

173. *Ezekiel 18:1-3 "God's Message to me: "What do you people mean by going around the country repeating the saying, The parents ate green apples, The children got the stomachache? "As* sure as I'm the living God, you're not going to repeat this saying in Israel any longer." (Message).

I decree and declare that I will not fight my parents' battle. I set myself free from every generational evil pattern. I separate myself and my children from any generational problem, sickness, and poverty.

174. *Job 22:27-28 "You will make your prayer to Him, He will hear you, and you will pay your vows. 28 You will also declare a thing, and it will be established for you; so light will shine on your ways." (NKJV).*

Father, I declare light to shine on my ways. I declare light to shine on the path of my children. My children will see what they ought to see in Jesus' name.

175. *Isaiah 60:11 "Therefore your gates shall be open continually; they shall not be shut day or night, that men may bring to you the wealth of the gentiles, and their kings in procession." (NKJV).*

Lord, in this land, doors of advancement shall never be shut against our children. Their gates shall continually be open, wealth shall come to them.

176. *2 Chronicles 7:14 "If My people who are called by My name will humble themselves, and pray and seek My face, and turn from their wicked ways, then I will hear from heaven, and I will forgive their sin and heal their land." (NKJV).*

Lord, have mercy on us in this nation. Lord be gracious unto us and heal our land.

The Church

THE Gate of hell is fighting to render the church ineffective; kingdomS of darkness lost that battle because the Lord himself WAS building his church. The church is in many ways the solution to the world problems. Let us stand together and pray for the church of our lord Jesus Christ. (Matthew 16:18). Let us pray!

177. *Matthew 10:1 "And when He had called His twelve disciples to Him, He gave them power over unclean spirits, to cast them out, and to heal all kinds of sickness and all kinds of disease." (NKJV).*

Lord, manifest your power in our church and use this church to destroy the satanic kingdom in this nation and all over the world, in the name of Jesus!

178. *Psalms 86:14-15 "O God, the proud have risen against me, And a mob of violent men have sought my life, and have not set You before them. But You, O Lord, are a God full of compassion, and gracious, long-suffering and abundant in mercy and truth." (NKJV).*

Father, I scatter every evil meeting summoned against the goal and the vision of our church, our pastors, and every member, in the name of Jesus.

179. *Isaiah 60: 22 "A little one shall become a thousand, and a small one a strong nation: I the Lord will hasten it in his time." (KJV).*

Father, pour upon us at this church Greater Grace, for unlimited Church Growth throughout this year. Supernaturally, increase us numerically, and let our impact spread into every soul in and around us!

180. *1 Corinthians 3:6 "My work was to plant the seed in your hearts, and Apollos' work was to water it, but it was God, not we, who made the garden grow in your hearts." (TLB).*

Father, throughout this year, let your WORD coming from this altar, prosper in my heart and profit my life.

181. *Jeremiah 1:19 "They will fight against you, but they shall not prevail against you. For I am with you, says the LORD, to deliver you." (NKJV).*

Father, I declare that every attack against our church, its members and our pastors, backfire, in the name of Jesus! We receive our victory in the name of Jesus!

182. *Ezra 6:3-4 "In the first year of King Cyrus, King Cyrus issued a decree concerning the house of God at Jerusalem: "Let the house be rebuilt, the place where they offered sacrifices; and let the foundations of it be firmly laid, its height sixty cubits and its width sixty cubits, with three rows of heavy stones and one row of new timber. Let the expenses be paid from the king's treasury." (NKJV).*

Father, complete our church building project, and let the expenses be paid from the King's treasury. Supply all the needed funds and send us financial Boaz in the name of Jesus!

183. 2 Chronicles 31:20 *"Thus Hezekiah did throughout all Judah, and he did what was good and right and true before the LORD his God." (NKJV).*

Father, help us to always do what is good, right. And true in your sight, as we serve you here at our church. Do not let us lose relevance, in the name of Jesus!

184. Matthew 16:18-19 *"And I also say to you that you are Peter, and on this rock I will build My church, and the gates of Hades shall not [g]prevail against it. And I will give you the keys of the kingdom of heaven, and whatever you bind on earth [h]will be bound in heaven, and whatever you loose on earth will be loosed in heaven." (NKJV).*

Father, we destroy every gang-up against the welfare and the growth of this church, in the name of Jesus! We crush every agenda of hell against the advancement of this church, in the name of Jesus!

185. Zechariah 2:3-5 *"And, behold, the angel that talked with me went forth, and another angel went out to meet him, And said unto him, Run, speak to this young man, saying, Jerusalem shall be inhabited as towns without walls for the multitude of men and cattle therein: For I, saith the Lord, will be unto her a wall of fire round about, and will be the glory in the midst of her." (KJV).*

Father, we declare that this church is a city without walls for the multitude of men and women trooping into worship & serve the

Lord in this place. This church, Your Growth and Your Glory, will know no bounds, in the name of Jesus Christ!

186. Acts 5:12 *"And through the hands of the apostles many signs and wonders were done among the people. And they were all with one accord in Solomon's porch." (NKJV).*

Father, in the name of Jesus, let there be a continuous eruption of miracles, signs, and wonders in all our services at this church, thereby drawing souls into the kingdom and into this church.

187. Act 11:21- *"And the hand of the Lord was with them, and a great number believed and turned to the Lord." (ESV).*

Father, in the name of Jesus, let your hand be upon us as we evangelize that people will believe and turn to you. With your fire burning through us, we will ignite the whole state and nation.

188. Isaiah 56:7 *"Even them I will bring to My holy mountain and make them joyful in My house of prayer. Their burnt offerings and their sacrifices will be accepted on My altar; For My house shall be called a house of prayer for all nations." (NKJV).*

Father, make this church your house of prayer for all nations, in Jesus Name; Make everyone that comes here joyful, and accept our offerings and sacrifices, in Jesus Name.

189. Acts 19: 11-12 *"Now God worked unusual miracles by the hands of Paul, so that even handkerchiefs or aprons were* *brought from his body to the sick, and the disease left them and the evil spirits went out of them." (NKJV).*

Father in the name of Jesus, saturate this church, the auditorium, grounds, and environment with your power, such that merely walking into it, will cause divine encounters. Healing, deliverance, and other miracles, signs, and wonders will continue to happen daily. These encounters will go round the world to draw men here to seek you in Jesus' name.

190. Matthew 10:1 "And when He had called His twelve disciples to Him, He gave them power over unclean spirits, to cast them out, and to heal all kinds of sickness and all kinds of disease." (NKJV).

Lord, reposition our church as a ministry, and use this church to destroy the satanic kingdom in this nation and all over the world, in the name of Jesus!

191. 2 Chronicles 31:20 "Thus Hezekiah did throughout all Judah, and he did what was good and right and true before the LORD his God." (NKJV).

Father, help us to always do what is good, right, and true in your sight, as we serve you here at our church.

192. Zephaniah 3:15 "The LORD has taken away your judgments, He has cast out your enemy. The King of Israel, The LORD, is in your midst; you shall see disaster no more." (NKJV).

Father, take away from our church any negative propaganda against us. Cast away all our enemies as you have promised. Rule in our midst, and let us see disaster no more, in the name of Jesus!

193. Exodus 36:5&7 "And they spoke to Moses, saying, "The people bring much more than enough for the service of the work which the Lord commanded us to do." .... for the material they had was sufficient for all the work to be done—indeed too much." (NKJV).

Father, supply all the finances, materials, and workers for the work of the new building. Let there be sufficiency and overflow, in the name of Jesus!

194. Psalms 85:6 "Will You not revive us again, that Your people may rejoice in You?" (Amplified).

Father, send down the fire of revival upon our church and make us your voice in this land!

195. Matthew 9:38 "Therefore pray The Lord of the harvest to send out laborers into His harvest." (NKJV).

Lord, bring the workers of Your choice to us and keep all other evil agents away, in the name of Jesus!

196. Psalms 68:30 "Rebuke our enemies, O Lord. Bring them— submissive, tax in hand. Scatter all who delight in war." (TLB).

Father, scatter those who delight in spreading evil reports about our church, our pastors, and leadership, bring them to their knees with your righteous judgment in the name of Jesus!

197. Zechariah 8:3 *"Thus says The Lord: "I will return to Zion, and dwell in the midst of Jerusalem. Jerusalem shall be called the City of Truth, The Mountain of The Lord of hosts, The Holy Mountain." (NKJV).*

Father return to our church in Your fullness, come and dwell in our midst and call our church the City of Truth in the name of Jesus.

198. 2 Corinthians 7:1 *"Therefore, having these promises, beloved, let us cleanse ourselves from all filthiness of the flesh and spirit, perfecting holiness in the fear of God." (NKJV).*

Lord, make our church a citadel of holiness, wonder, miracles, and glory upon the earth in the name of Jesus!

199. Exodus 14:21-22, *"Then Moses stretched out his hand over the sea; and the Lord caused the sea to go back by a strong east wind all that night, and made the sea into dry land, and the waters were divided. So, the children of Israel went into the midst of the sea on the dry ground, and the waters were a wall to them on their right hand and on their left." (NKJV).*

Father, the glory that moved Moses forward in the Red Sea, let it move our church, its leadership, and membership forward, in the name of Jesus!

200. *Psalms 115:14 "The LORD shall increase you more and more, you and your children." (KJV).*

Father, increase our church more and more in the name of Jesus! Increase us and our children more and more, and let the whole world see it.

201. *Psalms 68:28 "Your God has commanded your strength; Strengthen, O God, what You have done for us." (NKJV).*

Lord, let no man prevail against our church, its leadership, and membership, in the name of Jesus!

202. *2 Thessalonians 3:1-2; "Finally, brethren, pray for us, that the word of the Lord may run swiftly and be glorified, just as it is with you, and that we may be delivered from unreasonable and wicked men; for not all have faith." (NKJV).*

Father, let the Word of The Lord have free course and be glorified in our church and my life, in the name of Jesus!

203. *Jeremiah 31:14 "I will satiate the soul of the priests with abundance, and My people shall be satisfied with My goodness, says the LORD." (NKJV).*

Lord, satisfy our church, its members, and our pastors with abundance. Satisfy us with your goodness, in the name of Jesus!

204. *Psalms 85:6 "Will You not revive us again, that Your people may rejoice in You?"(Amplified).*

Father, send down the fire of revival upon our church, in the name of Jesus! From this year 2015 make us your voice in this land!

205. *1 Kings 6:14 "So Solomon finished building the Temple." (NLT).*

Father, finish and complete the church building project through the hands of your servants, our pastors, in the name of Jesus!

206. *Ezra 6:14 "So the elders of the Jews built, and they prospered through the prophesying of Haggai the prophet." (NKJV).*

Father, let every member of our church prosper greatly as they continue to build your church, in the name of Jesus.

207. *Ezekiel 43:12 "And this is the basic law of the Temple: absolute holiness! The entire top of the mountain where the Temple is built is holy. Yes, this is the basic law of the Temple." (NLT).*

Father, sanctify this new building as Your most holy place. Let Your presence and glory always fill the house.

208. *Psalms 68:19 "Blessed be The Lord, who daily loads us with benefits." (NKJV).*

Father, give us testimonies every day at our church for the glory of your name!

209. *Matthew 9:38 "Therefore pray The Lord of the harvest to send out laborers into His harvest." (NKJV).*

Lord, bring the workers of Your choice to our church, and keep all other evil agents away, in the name of Jesus!

210. *Exodus 36:5&7 "And they spoke to Moses, saying, "The people are bringing more than enough for doing this work that God has commanded us to do!" There was plenty of material for all the work to be done. Enough and more than enough." (Message).*

Father, supply all the finances, materials and workers for the work of the new building. Let there be sufficiency and overflow, in the name of Jesus!

211. *Deuteronomy 1:11 "May the Lord, the God of your ancestors, increase you a thousand times and bless you as He has promised!" (NKJV).*

Lord, increase our church a thousand times more, and bless us, in the name of Jesus!

212. *2 Corinthians 7:1 "Therefore, having these promises, beloved, let us cleanse ourselves from all filthiness of the flesh and spirit, perfecting holiness in the fear of God." (NKJV).*

Lord, make our church a citadel of holiness, wonder, miracles, and glory upon the earth, in the name of Jesus!

213. *Psalms 68:1-2 "God is already beginning to arise, and His enemies to scatter; let them also who hate Him flee before Him! As smoke is driven away, so drive them away; as wax melts before the fire, so let the wicked perish before the presence of God." (Amplified).*

Arise O God and scatter all the enemies of our church. Let those who plan evil against our church, and its members, be put to shame, in the name of Jesus!

214. *Exodus 33:18 "And he said, "Please show me Your glory." (NKJV).*

Father during this Convention, show us and manifest your glory in our midst and pour out your Spirit in greater measure into our lives, in the name of Jesus!

215. *1 Samuel 3:21 "God continued to show up at Shiloh, revealed through his word to Samuel at Shiloh." (Message).*

Father, appear again to us during this convention. Reveal Yourself to us through Your Word from all the speakers. Manifest Your presence through signs and wonders, in the name of Jesus!

216. *Mark 2:1-2 "After a few days, Jesus returned to Capernaum, and word got around that he was back home. 2 A crowd gathered, jamming the entrance so no one could get in or out. He was teaching the Word." (Message).*

Father, let the word go around that you are back home here at our church. Bring the crowd into our church and fill this house up. Release the WORD in season to us in the name of Jesus!

217. *2 Chronicles 2:5 "The house I am building has to be the best, for our God is the best, far better than competing gods." (Message).*

Father, complete the building of this house, make it the best; send us all the financial and human resources needed. Rest your beauty upon this house and make our church your resting place in the name of Jesus!

218.   Isaiah 33:20 *"Look upon Zion, the city of our appointed feasts; Your eyes will see Jerusalem, a quiet home, a Tabernacle that will not be taken down; not one of its stakes will ever be removed, nor will any of its cords be broken." (NKJV).*

Father, frustrate and cast down every power planning to wage war against the divine vision of our church, our pastors, and every member of our church in the name of Jesus!

219.   Mark 2:1-2 *"After a few days, Jesus returned to Capernaum, and word got around that he was back home. 2 A crowd gathered, jamming the entrance so no one could get in or out. He was teaching the Word." (Message).*

Father, let the word go around that you are back home here at our church. Bring the crowd into our church and fill this house up. Release the WORD in season to us in the name of Jesus!

220.   2 Chronicles 2:5 *"The house I am building has to be the best, for our God is the best, far better than competing gods." (Message).*

Father, complete the building of this house; make it the best; send us all the financial and human resources needed. Rest your beauty upon this house and make our church your resting place in the name of Jesus!

221. *Psalms 85:6 "Will You not revive us again, that Your people may rejoice in You?" (Amplified).*

Father, send down the fire of revival upon our church, in the name of Jesus! After these days of prayer and fasting, make us your voice in this land!

222. *Luke 8:17 "For nothing is secret that will not be revealed, nor anything hidden that will not be known and come to light." (NKJV).*

Lord, bring to light and expose everything planned in darkness, against our church, its members, and our pastor's family, in the name of Jesus!

223. *2 Chronicles 31:10 "And Azariah the high priest, from the family of Zadok, replied, "Since the people began bringing their gifts to the Lord's Temple, we have had enough to eat and plenty to spare. The Lord has blessed His people, and all this is left over." (NLT).*

Father, bless your people of our church as they continue to give to the completion of the building and prosper us greatly this year, in the name of Jesus!

224. *2 Chronicles 30:21 "And in every work that he began in the service of the house of God, in the law and in the commandment, to seek his God, he did it with all his heart, so he prospered." (NKJV).*

Father, as we seek You and serve you with all our hearts at this church, prosper us and do not let our labor and service be in vain. Remember us for good, in the name of Jesus!

225. *Isaiah 49:26 "And your enemies, crazed and desperate, will turn on themselves, killing each other in a frenzy of self-destruction. Then everyone will know that I, God, have saved you—I, the Mighty One of Jacob." (Message).*

Father, I declare, any power planning untimely death for me this year, die in my place, in the name of Jesus!

226. *Hebrews 6:3 "And so, God willing, we will move forward to further understanding." (NLT).*

Father, I break myself loose from the bondage of life stagnation, I shall move forward; and I reverse every evil arrangement setup for my life, in the name of Jesus!

227. *Zechariah 8:3 "Thus says The Lord: "I will return to Zion, and dwell amid Jerusalem. Jerusalem shall be called the City of Truth, The Mountain of The Lord of hosts, The Holy Mountain." (NKJV).*

Father, send down the fire of revival upon our church in the name of Jesus! Let miracles, signs and wonders be daily occurrences and make us your voice in this land!

228. *Exodus 36:5&7 "And they spoke to Moses, saying, "The people are bringing more than enough for doing this work that God has commanded us to do!" ... There was plenty of material* for all the work to be done. Enough and more than enough."(Message).

Father, supply all the finances, materials and workers for the completion of this new building. Let there be sufficiency and overflow in the name of Jesus!

229. *2 Thessalonians 3:1-2; "Finally, brethren, pray for us, that the word of the Lord may run swiftly and be glorified, just as it is with you, and that we may be delivered from unreasonable and wicked men; for not all have faith." (NKJV).*

Father, let the Word of The Lord have free course and be glorified in our church and my life, in the name of Jesus!

230. *Psalms 115:14 "The LORD shall increase you more and more, you and your children." (NKJV).*

Father, increase our church more and more, in the name of Jesus! Increase us and our children more and more, and let the whole world see it.

231. *Jeremiah 31:14 "I will satiate the soul of the priests with abundance, and My people shall be satisfied with My goodness, says the LORD." (NKJV).*

Lord, satisfy our church, its members, and our pastors with abundance. Satisfy us with your goodness in the name of Jesus!

232. *Psalms 28:4 "They talk a good line of "peace," then moonlight for the Devil. Pay them back for what they've done, for how bad they've been. Pay them back for their long hours in* the Devil's workshop; Then cap it with a huge bonus." (Message).

Father, visit those who are plotting against our church and its members with the same plot they are planning. Reward them with a huge bonus of their evil plots, in the name of Jesus!

233. Isaiah 17:14 *"Then behold, at eventide, trouble! And before the morning, he is no more. This is the portion of those who plunder us, and the lot of those who rob us."(NKJV).*

Father, frustrate and remove anything or anyone that wants to make our church lose relevance and impact home and abroad, in the name of Jesus!

234. Exodus 33:18 *"And he said, "Please show me Your glory." (NKJV).*

Father, manifest your glory in our midst and pour out your Spirit in greater measure in our lives. May we encounter the manifestation of your presence, heavenly encounters, signs, and wonders!

235. 1 Peter 2:4 *"Welcome to the living Stone, the source of life. The workmen took one look and threw it out; God set it in the place of honor." (Message).*

Father, set our pastors up in the place of honor. Where they have been rejected, give them a place of honor. Let those who have worked against them begin to work for them. Let those that hated them begin to celebrate them, in the name of Jesus!

236. Revelation 3:11 *"I'm on my way; I'll be there soon. Keep a tight grip on what you have so no one distracts you and steals your crown." (Message).*

Father, disgrace and destroy anything or anyone trying to distract me to steal my crown, my peace, my joy, and my relevance, in the name of Jesus!

237. Jeremiah 30:19 *"Then out of them shall proceed thanksgiving and the voice of those who make merry; I will multiply them, and they shall not diminish; I will also glorify them, and they shall not be small. (NKJV).*

We demolish every artificial ceiling placed upon the growth of our church, in the name of Jesus. We nullify and cancel every curse pronounced on our church to limit growth in the name of Jesus.

238. Zephaniah 3:15 *"The LORD has taken away your judgements, He has cast out your enemy. The King of Israel, The LORD, is in your midst; you shall see disaster no more." (NKJV).*

Father, take away from our church any judgment against us. Cast away all our enemies as you have promised. Rule in our midst throughout this year and let us see no disaster, in the name of Jesus!

239. Acts 2:5-6 *"There were some religious Jews staying in Jerusalem who were from every country in the world. 6 When they heard this noise, a crowd came together. They were all surprised, because each one heard them speaking in his own language. (NCV).*

Father, we declare that this church is a church for all nations and people. Let The Holy Spirit manifest in our midst, so that all will hear their language each time they come to service. Speak in this church, the language of healing, prosperity, deliverance, wisdom, financial strength, in the name of Jesus.

240. *Isaiah 33:20 "Look upon Zion, the city of our appointed feasts; Your eyes will see Jerusalem, a quiet home, a Tabernacle that will not be taken down; not one of its stakes will ever be removed, nor will any of its cords be broken." (NKJV).*

Father, frustrate and cast down every power planning to wage war against the divine vision of our church, our pastors, and members, in the name of Jesus!

241. *Mark 2:1-2 "After a few days, Jesus returned to Capernaum, and word got around that he was back home. 2 A crowd gathered, jamming the entrance so no one could get in or out. He was teaching the Word." (Message).*

Father, let the word go around that you are back home, here at our church. Bring the crowd into our church and fill this house up. Release the WORD in season to us in the name of Jesus!

242. *Deuteronomy 1:11 "May the Lord God of your fathers make you a thousand times more numerous than you are and bless you as He has promised you!" (NKJV).*

Father, increase our church a thousand times more in the name of Jesus! Increase us and our children more and more, and make us your voice in this land, in the name of Jesus!

243. *Isaiah 5:26 "He will send a signal to distant nations far away and whistle to those at the ends of the earth. They will come racing toward Jerusalem. (NLT).*

Father, blow your whistle far to the ends of the earth and in this city where you located us, and let the people come racing towards this church and give us a harvest of souls, in the name of Jesus.

244. *Acts 2:5-6 "At that time there were devout Jews from every nation living in Jerusalem. 6 When they heard the loud noise, everyone came running, and they were bewildered to hear their own languages being spoken by the believers." (NLT).*

Father, make your presence at this church known all over this city and nation, so that people of all races come to this church. Let everyone hear their language (healing, deliverance, financial prosperity or whatever they need to hear) each time they come to the service, in the name of Jesus.

245. *Nehemiah 6:15-16 "So on October 2 the wall was finished— When our enemies and the surrounding nations heard about it, they were frightened and humiliated. They realized this work had been done with the help of our God." (NLT).*

Father, complete the work of this church building, so that when people see and hear about it they will know that God was behind this work, in the name of Jesus. Give us strength, financially, to complete the beautification of this building, in the name of Jesus.

246. *Exodus 4:31 "So the people believed; and when they heard that the LORD had visited the children of Israel and that He had looked on their affliction, then they bowed their heads and worshiped." (NKJV).*

Father, visit us again as a church and let the news spread all over the world that you are with us. Manifest your presence with miracles, signs and wonders, in the name of Jesus.

247. *Revelation 11:11 "Now after the three-and-a-half days the breath of life from God entered them, and they stood on their feet, and great fear fell on those who saw them." (NKJV).*

Father, breathe on us again. Let everyone that is sick be back on their feet. Lift us back on our feet spiritually, physically, emotionally, and financially, in the name of Jesus.

248. *Isaiah 28:5 "Then at last the Lord Almighty himself will be their crowning glory, the diadem of beauty to his people who are left." (TLB).*

Father, show yourself as the crowning glory of this church. Let the diadem of your beauty reflect on our family and let the world see it. This church will no longer be hidden, in the name of Jesus.

249. *Isaiah 52:1 "Wake up! Open your eyes! Beautiful Zion, put on your majestic strength! Jerusalem, the sacred city, put on* *your glory garments! Never again will the unclean enter your gates!" (TPT).*

Father, we declare that after this Convention, our strength will be renewed, and nothing UNCLEAN will enter our lives again, in the name of Jesus. Your strength will become our strength and our glory garment will radiate all around the world, in the name of Jesus.

250. Isaiah 49:12 "Look! They will come from faraway lands—some from the north, some from the west, and some from the land of Sinim." (TPT).

Father, we declare an increase for this church during this Convention, in the name of Jesus. Let people come from faraway lands – from north, from the south, east and west of this land in the name of Jesus. Visit us in an unusual way during this Celebration and announce your presence in our mist through miracles, signs, and wonders, in the name of Jesus.

251. Esther 8:17 "In each and every province and in each and every city, wherever the king's command and his decree arrived, the Jews celebrated with gladness and joy, a feast and a holiday. And many among the peoples of the land became Jews, for the fear of the Jews (and their God) had fallen on them." (Amplified).

Father, let the fear of your doings at this church fall on this land and gain souls for yourself, in the mighty name of Jesus! Lord, make this church the tabernacle of celebration, gladness, and joy, in the mighty name of Jesus!

252. Ezra 5: 4-5 *"They also asked the Jews for the names of the men who were working on this building. 5. But the leaders of the Jews were under God's watchful eye. They couldn't be stopped until Dairus received a report and sent a reply to it." (God's Word Translation).*

Father, let the leaders of this church be under the perpetual God's watchful eye. Lord, watch over our pastors, and every family represented at this church, in the mighty name of Jesus! Let nothing stop us from achieving God's purpose and counsel for our lives. The enemy will not be able to stop or hinder our wives, children, husbands from prospering.

253. Nehemiah 2:20 *"So I answered them, and said to them, "The God of heaven Himself will prosper us; therefore, we His servants will arise and build, but you have no heritage or right or memorial in Jerusalem." (NKJV).*

Father, we declare that on this mountain, from this day forward, the God of heaven Himself will prosper every member of this church, in the mighty name of Jesus! We will not be weary, tired or discouraged in the race of life. God will prosper the work of our hands, our families, our church, and pastors, in the mighty name of Jesus!

254. Proverbs 14:34 *"Righteousness exalts a nation, But sin is a reproach to any people." (NKJV).*

We cry for help; deliver every nation from every reproach of sin. Set your face of mercy and compassion upon us all as a people; let righteousness reign!

255. *Matthew 16:18 "And I also say to you that you are Peter, and on this rock I will build My church, and the gates of Hades shall not prevail against it. 19 And I will give you the keys of the kingdom of heaven, and whatever you bind on earth I will be bound in heaven, and whatever you loose on earth will be loosed in heaven." (NKJV).*

Father, we pray that this church is built upon Jesus, the rock. Therefore the gates of hell will not prevail over us, enemies will not prevail over us, afflictions shall not prevail over us, evil shall not prevail over us, devil and all his cohort shall not prevail over us, in the mighty name of Jesus Christ.

256. *Acts 2:47 "Praising God continually and having favor with all the people. And the Lord kept adding to their number daily those who were being saved." (Amplified).*

Father, reposition our church to the status of Favor with all men! Help your Church to do what is right. Let your Church have once again, one voice!

257. *Psalms 80:19 "Restore us, O Lord God of hosts, cause Your face to shine, And we shall be saved." (NKJV).*

Father, restore our families, homes, ministries, and the church that we will always be the light and love of the world, in Jesus' name. Thank you for making your face shine on our families, homes, ministries, and everything that concerns us so that we will continue to make a positive impact.

258. *2 Timothy 4:2 "Preach the word! Be ready in season and out of season, convince, rebuke, exhort with all longsuffering and teaching." (NKJV).*

Father, help us as a church to proclaim Your truth and preach your message in season and out of season in Jesus' name. We thank you because your word is life to us, use your word to rebuke us, correct us, and encourage us, so that we will not fall by the wayside.

Family

The lord is particular about you and your family. The lord who increased you is able, more than able to preserve, protect, provide and promote your family as well. Stand in the gap and pray for yourself, your immediate, and extended family.

"here I AM and the children whom the lord has given me, we are for signs and wonders…" (Isaiah 8:18). Let us pray!

259. *Numbers 31:49 "They told Moses, "We, your servants, have counted our soldiers under our command, and not one of them is missing." (TLB).*

Father, as we approach the end of this year, let no one be missing in my home, my church, my family, in the name of Jesus. Increase us and don't let us diminish, in the name of Jesus.

260. *Psalms 45:11 "So the King will greatly desire your beauty; Because He is your Lord, worship Him. (NKJV).*

Father, let your beauty be revealed in my life, in my home, in my children, in my finances and over my work, and let the World see it, in the name of Jesus!

261. *Deuteronomy 1:11 "May the Lord God of your fathers make you a thousand times more numerous than you are and bless you as He has promised you!" (NKJV).*

Father, increase this church a thousand times more in the name of Jesus! Increase us and our children more and more and make us your voice in this land, in the name of Jesus!

262. *1 Chronicles 29:2 "Using every resource at my command, I have gathered as much as could for building the Temple of my God. Now there is enough gold, silver, bronze, iron and wood, as well as great quantities of onyx, other precious stones, costly jewels, and all kinds of fine stone and marble." (NLT).*

Lord, we command an abundance of resources to come in for the finishing of the church building. Let there be enough and leftover money and resources to finish this project, in the name of Jesus!

263. *Exodus 36:5 "And they spoke to Moses, saying, "The people bring much more than enough for the service of the work which the Lord commanded us to do." (NKJV).*

Lord, touch your people to give to this work, so that it is enough and let there be leftovers, in the name of Jesus!

264. *Proverbs 11:29 "Exploit or abuse your family and end up with a fistful of air; common sense tells you it's a stupid way to live." (Message).*

Father, we declare healing for families all over the world. Lord, strengthen homes and families with peace and unity. We stand against every spirit that is breaking families apart, in the name of Jesus!

265. *Isaiah 54:13 "All your children shall be taught by the LORD, and great shall be the peace of your children." (NKJV).*

Father God, we ask for your protection over our children. Let no trouble fall on them, keeping them away from accidents. Allow no evil to influence their hearts. Cover them with the precious blood of Christ. Take charge over them so that they do not follow the crowd to do evil.

266. *Isaiah 54: 13-14 "All your children shall be taught by the Lord, And great shall be the peace of your children. In righteousness you shall be established, you shall be far from oppression for you shall not fear; And from terror, for it shall not come near you." (NKJV).*

Father, teach our children yourself and grant them great peace. Establish them in righteousness, let them be far from oppression, and let no terror come near them, in Jesus' Name.

267. *Psalms 143: 10-11 "You are my God. Show me what you want me to do, and let your gentle spirit lead me in the right path. Be true to your name Lord, and keep my life safe. Use your saving power to protect me from trouble." (CEV).*

Father, we present our children to you, please show them what you want them to do in this confusing world. Let your gentle spirit guide them in the right path and keep their lives safe, protect them from trouble by your saving power in Jesus Name.

268. *Isaiah 22: 21 "I will clothe him with your robe and strengthen him with your belt; I will commit your responsibility* *into his hand. He shall be a father to the inhabitants of Jerusalem and to the house of Judah." (NKJV).*

Father, in the name of Jesus, clothe our bishop with your robe, strengthen him with your belt, and make him a father to this nation and beyond. Continue to use him mightily for your glory, in Jesus Name.

269. Philippians 2:13 *"For it is God who works in you both to will and to do for His good pleasure." (NKJV).*

Father, I come against every work of the flesh, limiting the place of God inside me. I take grace to be God-inside-minded, Christ-minded, God pleaser, WORD-addict, Love-controlled, Soul-winner!

270. Romans 12:1-2 *"I beseech you therefore, brethren, by the mercies of God, that you present your bodies a living sacrifice, holy, acceptable to God, which is your reasonable service. 2 And do not be conformed to this world, but be transformed by the renewing of your mind, that you may prove what is that good and acceptable and perfect will of God." (NKJV).*

Father, I receive new capacity to be committed to the Practice of the WORD of God! I break myself loose from the cycle of self-deception, into a lifestyle of Prompt Obedience to the Lord and his commands.

271. Revelation 3:12 *"Then I'll write names on you, the pillars: the Name of my God, the Name of God's City—the new Jerusalem coming down out of Heaven—and my new Name." (Message).*

Father, write new names on me, my spouse, my children and my church. Where we have been called sick, let them call us healed; where we have been called poor, let them call us rich; where we have been called ordinary, let them call us great, in the name of Jesus!

272. *Nehemiah 9:24 – Their children went in and took possession of the land. You subdued before them the Canaanites, who lived in the land; you gave the Canaanites into their hands, along with their kings and the peoples of the land, to deal with them as they pleased. (NIV).*

Father, let my children take possession of this land and deliver their enemies into their hands, in the name of Jesus. Make my children second to nobody, in the name of Jesus!

273. *Jeremiah 31:29 "In those days they shall say no more: "The Fathers have eaten sour grapes, and the children's teeth are set on edge." (NKJV).*

Father, I declare that from today, the failure that happened in the lives of my parents will not happen in my life and in the lives of my children, in the name of Jesus!

274. *Psalms 119:173 "Put your hand out and steady me since I've chosen to live by your counsel." (Message).*

Father, reach out your hand and steady me and let nothing shake or destabilize me, my home, or my work, in the name of Jesus.

275. *Psalms 30:1 "I give you credit, GOD – you got me out of that mess, you didn't let my foes gloat." (Message).*

Father, we thank you for your protection over my family, children, health, career, and my church since the beginning of this year. Thank you for not allowing our enemies to rejoice over us.

276. *Psalms 31:21 "Praise the Lord, for He has shown me the wonders of his unfailing love. He kept me safe when my city was under attack." (NLT).*

Father, I praise you for keeping me, my family, my church and all that surrounds me safe from January to December. Thank you for keeping me safe from the attacks of the enemies.

277. *Psalms 115:14-15 "God himself will fill you with more. Blessings upon blessings will be heaped upon you and upon your children from the maker of heaven and earth, the very God who made you!" (Passion).*

Father, I declare, this year, I and my children receive blessings upon blessings with unrivaled liftings. I declare that my children excel in all they do, in the name of Jesus.

278. *Psalms 50:2 "Out of Zion, the perfection of beauty, God will shine forth." (NKJV).*

Father, shine forth with new strength in my life, in the life of my spouse, my children, work, business, career, and church, in the mighty name of Jesus! I receive the beauty of God in me, and everyone that sees me will see this beauty and glorify God.

279. *Psalms 32:8 "I hear the Lord saying, "I will stay close to you, instructing and guiding you along the pathway for your life. I will advise you along the way and lead you forth with my eyes as your guide." (TPT).*

Father, don't be far from our children, instruct our children and guide them along the pathway of their lives. Please God, teach and lead them the way they should go. Guide them with your eyes continually, in the mighty name of Jesus.

280. *Genesis 12: 2-3 "I will make you a great nation; I will bless you And make your name great; And you shall be a blessing. I will bless those who bless you, And I will curse him who curses you; And in you all the families of the earth shall be blessed." (NKJV).*

Heavenly Father, we thank and we bless your name for your favor and blessings over our health, lives, families, ministries, businesses, and professions. Father, we ask that You bless us, that you will make us a channel of blessing to others, just as we have received freely from you, in Jesus' name.

281. *2 Timothy 1: 7 "For God has not given us a spirit of fear, but of power and of love and of a sound mind." (NKJV).*

Father, you are the possessor of all knowledge and wisdom, in your mercy grant us divine wisdom as we make strategic and tactical decisions concerning all areas of our lives. Father, shut every false open door and unlock every door of blessings, which profit mightily with no sorrow whatsoever added, in Jesus' name.

282. Psalms 127:4 *"Like arrows in the hand of a warrior, So are the children of one's youth." (NKJV).*

Father, make our children arrows and no sorrows, in the name of Jesus!

283. John 10:5 *"And a stranger will they not follow, but will flee from him: for they know not the voice of strangers." (KJV).*

Father, there are many voices out there; we sanctify the hearing of our children. Keep our children from contrary and wicked voices.

284. 1 Chronicles 11:14 *"But they stationed themselves in the middle of that field, defended it, and killed the Philistines. So the Lord brought about a great victory." (NKJV).*

Father, make your word a tool of defense for our families against all devices of the wicked!

285. Joshua 24:15 *"And if it seem evil unto you to serve the LORD, choose you this day whom ye will serve; whether the gods which your fathers served that were on the other side of the flood, or the gods of the Amorites, in whose land ye dwell: but as for me and my house, we will serve the LORD." (KJV).*

Father, help me and my family to serve you with delight. Holy Spirit we surrender the affairs of our homes to you.

286. Psalms 90:14 *"O satisfy us early with thy mercy; that we may rejoice and be glad all our days." (KJV).*

Father, satisfy our children early. Oh Lord, bless their studies, for those who are working Lord, bless their career, for those who are married, bless their homes, for those who are getting married, bless their marriages, for those who are trusting God for a life partner, bless them with a godly life partner, that they may rejoice and be glad all their days, in Jesus mighty name.

287.   2 Timothy 3:14-15 "But you must continue in the things which you have learned and been assured of, knowing from whom you have learned them, and that from childhood you have known the Holy Scriptures, which are able to make you wise for salvation through faith which is in Christ Jesus." (NKJV).

Father, deliver our children from the lies of the world through social media and peer pressure, and make them hold on to what they have learned from the word of God through which they receive wisdom for a righteous living, in the mighty name of Jesus Christ.

288.   Psalms 73:26 "My flesh and my heart fail; But God is the strength of my heart and my portion forever." (NKJV).

Father, we pray for every family in this church. Be our strength in every area where we are weak (financially, emotionally, etc.). Rekindle the relationship between husbands and wives. Inject new love into our families. Be our portion now and forever, in the mighty name of Jesus.

289.   Psalms 16: 8 "I have set the Lord always before me; because He is at my right hand I shall not be moved." (KJV).

Father, we thank you for you are always at our right hand. You are the one that rules in our family affairs. Lord, we pray, let your praise be on our lips through thick and thin. Whatever comes our way, we will not be moved, in the mighty name of Jesus Christ.

290. *Psalms 127:3 "Behold children are a heritage from the Lord. The fruit of the womb is a reward." (NKJV).*

Father, we pray for your protection over our children. You are their hiding place, and under your wings they shall continuously find refuge in Jesus' name. We thank you for not making them ashamed, protecting them from trouble wherever they go, and keeping evil far from them.

291. *Proverbs 4: 23 "Keep your heart with all diligence, for out of it springs the issues of life." (NKJV).*

Lord, I pray my children's minds will be protected from evil and they will make wise choices in the face of peer pressure, in Jesus' name. We thank you that our children in this church will never perish, and no one will snatch them out of your hand.

Protection

GOD IS COMMITTED TO YOUR PROTECTION AND THE PROTECTION OF YOUR POSSESSIONS AND EVERYONE AROUND YOU. YOU ARE PROTECTED WHEN YOU GO OUT, WHEN YOU COME IN, WHEN YOU LAY DOWN, WHEN YOU WAKE UP. YOUR CHILDREN AT SCHOOL, YOUR PARENTS AT WORK, WHEN YOU TRAVEL BY ROAD, BY AIR, BY SEA OR BY RAIL, THE PROTECTION OF THE LORD IS YOURS.

PRAY AND RECEIVE GOD'S PROTECTION BECAUSE YOU DWELL IN THE SECRET PLACE OF THE MOST HIGH, AND YOU ABIDE UNDER THE SHADOW OF THE ALMIGHTY. (PSALMS 91:1). LET US PRAY!

292. *Job 5:12 "He frustrates the devices of the crafty, so that their hands cannot carry out their plans." (NKJV).*

Lord, build a wall of protection around our pastors and their children, in the name of Jesus. Let every plan against them be frustrated, in the name of Jesus.

293. *Jeramiah 1: 19 "They will fight against you, But they shall not prevail against you. For I am with you," says the LORD, "to deliver you." (NKJV).*

Father, thank you for your protection and security over our senior pastor and his family. The arm of flesh and its machinations will never prevail against him and his family.

Father, thank you because You will cause your righteous right hand to protect, secure, and uphold our senior pastors in Jesus' name.

294. Isaiah 33:24 *"And the inhabitant will not say, "I am sick"; The people who dwell in it will be forgiven their iniquity"* (NKJV).

Father, protect me and every member of our church and the leadership from sickness, affliction and death. Let no one amongst us say, "I am sick." Let us enjoy divine health continually, in the name of Jesus!

295. Psalms 16: 9-10 *"I'm happy from the inside out, and from the outside in, I'm firmly formed. You canceled my ticket to hell—that's not my destination!"* (Message).

Father, I cancel today every grave dug for anyone in this church. I declare that no one will die in our midst, in the name of Jesus!

296. Job 5:12 *"He frustrates the devices of the crafty, so that their hands cannot carry out their plans."* (NKJV).

Lord, build a wall of protection around our pastors and their children, in the name of Jesus. Let every plan against them be frustrated, in the name of Jesus!

297. 2 Samuel 1:19 *"Your pride and joy, O Israel, lies dead on the hills! Oh, how the mighty heroes have fallen!"* (NLT).

Father, my family is my pride and joy. Lord, protect us by your hand. Do not let any of my pride and joys die, however, destroy all the devices and plans of the devil against my pride and joys, in the name of Jesus!

298. *1 Kings 5:4 But now the Lord my God hath given me rest on every side, so that there is neither adversary nor evil occurrent. (KJV).*

Father, we thank you for the safety and peace you granted our city this week! We declare a greater atmosphere of peace, calmness and progress all over our cities, our states, and our country. Father we declare divine protection over all our officers: Law Enforcement, Fire Department, and First responders, in Jesus' name.

299. *Numbers 31:49 "They told Moses, "We, your servants, have counted our soldiers under our command, and not one of them is missing." (TLB).*

Father, as we enter 2015, let no one be missing in my home, my church, my family, in the name of Jesus. Increase us and don't let us diminish in the name of Jesus.

300. *Psalms 46:1 "God is our refuge and strength, A very present help in trouble." (NKJV).*

Father be my refuge this year, do not let me see evil. Protect me, my home, my children, any of my family members from an untimely death, in the name of Jesus.

301. *Hebrews 13:12 "Jesus himself suffered outside the city gate, so that his blood would make people holy." (CEV).*

Blood of Jesus, laminate my life in the name of Jesus!

302. *Isaiah 33:24 "And the inhabitant will not say, "I am sick"; The people who dwell in it will be forgiven their iniquity" (NKJV).*

Father, protect me and every member of this church from sickness, affliction, and death. Let no one amongst us say, "I am sick." Let us enjoy divine health continually, in the name of Jesus!

303. *Numbers 31:49 "They told Moses, "We, your servants, have counted our soldiers under our command, and not one of them is missing." (TLB).*

Father, as we approach the end of this year, let no one be missing in my home, my church, my family, in the name of Jesus. Increase us and don't let us diminish in the name of Jesus.

304. *Psalms 68:28 "Summon your might; display your strength, O God, for you have done such mighty things for us." (TLB).*

Father, display your strength in my life, my home, my work, my ministry, my family, and my church and let me not be put to shame. Establish me for greatness, in the name of Jesus.

305. *1 Peter 1:5. "God is keeping careful watch over us and the future. The Day is coming when you'll have it all—life healed and whole." (Message).*

Father, let the great and prosperous future that you have for me begin today. Let my present show the preview of my future and make the whole world concur that your hand is upon my life, in the name of Jesus!

306. *Psalms 68:19-20 " What a glorious Lord! He who daily bears our burdens also gives us our salvation. He frees us! He rescues us from death." (TLB).*

Father, I cast my burdens on you. Set me free from the spirit of fear and worry, in the name of Jesus. Rescue me from the traps of death laid for me by the evil ones, in the name of Jesus.

307. *Psalms 119:173 "Put your hand out and steady me since I've chosen to live by your counsel." (Message).*

Father, reach out your hand and steady me and let nothing shake or destabilize me in my home and work, in the name of Jesus.

308. *Isaiah 49:23 "Kings will be your babysitters; princesses will be your nursemaids. They'll offer to do all your drudge work—scrub your floors, do your laundry. You'll know then that I am God. No one who hopes in me ever regrets it." (Message).*

Father, send us help in unlikely places in the name of Jesus! Bring help from governments, from corporations, from individuals and businesses, in the name of Jesus!

309. *Nehemiah 9:21 – Yea, forty years didst thou sustain them in the wilderness, so that they lacked nothing; their clothes waxed not old, and their feet swelled not. (KJV).*

Father, sustain me for the rest of my life. Let my life bring glory to your name and remove shame far from me and my family, in the name of Jesus!

310. Revelation 12:10 *"Then I heard a loud voice saying in heaven, "Now salvation, and strength, and the kingdom of our God, and the power of His Christ have come, for the accuser of our brethren, who accused them before our God day and night, has been cast down." (NKJV).*

Father, I declare that from today, I begin to enjoy in double portions, salvation, strength and the power of Christ in the name of Jesus! All my accusers are silenced, in the name of Jesus!

311. *1 Peter 2:4. "Welcome to the Living Stone, the source of life. The workmen took one look and threw it out; God set it in the place of honor." (Message).*

Father, set my pastors up in the place of honor. Where they have been rejected, give them a place of honor there. Let those who have worked against them, begin to work for them. Let those that hated them, begin to celebrate them, in the name of Jesus!

312. *Luke 1:25 "Thus the Lord has dealt with me, in the days when He looked on me, to take away my reproach among people." (NKJV).*

Father, from today, take away my reproach. Look down upon me and cause your favor to rest upon my household, in the name of Jesus!

313. *Psalms 119:16 "Take my side as you promised; I'll live then for sure. Don't disappoint all my grand hopes." (Message).*

Father, bring to pass every promise you have given to me and cause me to give testimonies, in the name of Jesus!

314. *Revelation 12:7-8; "And war broke out in heaven: Michael and his angels fought with the dragon; and the dragon and his angels fought, but they did not prevail, nor was a place found for them in heaven any longer." (NKJV).*

Father, I declare from today, no place will be found for Satan in my life, my home, my ministry, my family, my finances, or my church, in the name of Jesus!

315. *Revelation 3:11 "I'm on my way; I'll be there soon. Keep a tight grip on what you have so no one distracts you and steals your crown. (Message).*

Father, disgrace and destroy anything or anyone trying to distract me to steal my crown, my peace, my joy, or my relevance, in the name of Jesus!

316. *Revelation 3:12 "Then I'll write names on you, the pillars: the Name of my God, the Name of God's City—the new Jerusalem coming down out of Heaven—and my new Name." (Message).*

Father, write new names on me, my spouse, my children and my church! Where we have been called sick, let them call us healed; where we have been called poor, let them call us rich;

where we have been called ordinary, let them call us great, in the name of Jesus!

317. *Isaiah 54:17 "No weapon formed against you shall prosper, and every tongue which rises against you in judgment You shall condemn. This is the heritage of the servants of the LORD, and their righteousness is from Me." (NKJV).*

Father, destroy every satanic device employed or intended to be employed against any member Kingdom Connection Christian Center and their family, in the form of death, victimization, insanity, accident, and any other means, in the name of Jesus!

318. *Numbers 31:49 "They told Moses, "We, your servants, have counted our soldiers under our command, and not one of them is missing." (TLB).*

Father, as we approach the end of this year, let no one be missing in my home, my church, my family, in the name of Jesus. Increase us and don't let us diminish, in the name of Jesus.

319. *Proverbs 23:18 "You will be rewarded for this; your hope will not be disappointed." (NLT).*

Father, do not let my hope be disappointed in life, so reward me with abundance, in the name of Jesus.

320. *Ezra 7:6 "This Ezra was a scribe who was well versed in the Law of Moses, which the Lord, the God of Israel, had given to the people of Israel. He came up to Jerusalem from Babylon, and the king gave him everything he asked for, because the gracious hand of the Lord his God was on him." (NKJV).*

Father, let your hand of favor be upon my life and terminate my labor and toiling in the name of Jesus.

321. *1 Samuel 30:9-10 "David went, he and the six hundred men with him. They arrived at the Brook Besor, where some of them dropped out. David and four hundred men kept up the pursuit, but two hundred of them were too fatigued to cross the Brook Besor, and stayed there." (Message).*

Father, don't let me drop out in the battle of life, let your Holy Spirit build me up and give me strength in the name of Jesus. Give me strength to pray, to read the Word and walk in obedience to the WORD, strength to be faithful in all areas of my life.

322. *Psalms 18:20 "God made my life complete when I placed all the pieces before him. When I got my act together, he gave me a fresh start. (Message).*

Father, I place my life before you, every piece of it. Make my life complete this year, lacking nothing, in the name of Jesus.

323. *Psalms 18:28 "Suddenly, God, you floodlight my life; I'm blazing with glory, God's glory! (Message).*

Father, floodlight my life from today and let me be blazing with your glory in this year of shining glory. Let your glory shine through my life, finances, health, home, work, children, church, and city in the name of Jesus.

324. *John 10:5 "They won't follow stranger's voice but will scatter because they aren't used to the sound of it." (Message).*

Father, we declare your protection over our children. They will not follow a stranger's voice; they will prosper and serve you all their days in the name of Jesus.

325. Psalms 118:16-17 *"The right hand of the Lord is exalted; The right hand of the Lord does valiantly. I shall not die, but live, and declare the works of the Lord. (NKJV).*

Father, let the angels of deliverance that have been stationed around this place, now, let them be laying their hands on anyone here that has been having dreams of death, in the name of Jesus!

326. Psalms 18:36 *"You cleared the ground under me so my footing was firm." (Message).*

Father, hold me firmly and let nothing pull me down. Set my footing firmly on your word and make me an example of the power of your word, in the name of Jesus.

327. Psalms 46:1 *"God, you're such a safe and powerful place to find refuge! You're a proven help in time of trouble— more than enough and always available whenever I need you. (Passion).*

Father, be my refuge this year, do not let me see evil. Protect me, my home, my children, and all my family members from untimely death, in the name of Jesus.

328. Numbers 31:49 *"We have counted the soldiers under our command and not a man is missing." (Message).*

Father, as we approach the middle of this year, let no one be missing in this church, my home, my family, in the name of Jesus. Increase us and don't let us diminish, in the name of Jesus. Stretch Your hand and heal all who are sick amongst us in the name of Jesus.

329. *2 Chronicles 7:14 "If my people, which are called by my name, shall humble themselves, and pray and seek my face, and turn from their wicked ways; then I will hear from heaven, and will forgive their sins, and will heal their land." (NKJV).*

Father, as we pray individually and cooperatively today, hear and answer our prayers for revival in this nation and all over the world in Jesus' name. We thank You for healing the land and, we ask you to bring peace to the country of United States, Ukraine, and the entire world.

330. *Psalms 46:1 "God is our refuge and strength. A very present help in trouble." (NKJV).*

Father, we lift the hands of our senior pastor, his wife, and their children and always place them in your shelter in Jesus' name. We thank you because we know that you are their refuge and fortress, and you will preserve them all the time.

Divine Healing

Earthly ministry of Jesus Christ is often punctuated by miracles of healing, restoration and deliverance from sickness, diseases and death. Divine healing is still available today. Healing is children's bread. Ask for yourself and you will have, ask for others and they will receive.

"Beloved, I pray that you may prosper in all things and be in health, just as your soul prospers" (3 John 1:2) Let us pray for divine healing!

331. *Jeremiah 30:17 "For I will restore health unto thee, and I will heal thee of thy wounds, saith the LORD; because they called thee an Outcast, saying, this is Zion, whom no man seeketh after." (KJV).*

Father, we release your healing virtue on everyone sick in our midst. Restore health to them and heal them completely, in the name of Jesus!

332. *Psalms 68:19-20 " What a glorious Lord! He who daily bears our burdens also gives us our salvation. He frees us! He rescues us from death." (TLB).*

Father, I cast my burdens on you, set me free from the spirit of fear and worry in the name of Jesus. Rescue me from the traps of death laid for me by the evil ones in the name of Jesus.

333. *Psalms 16: 9-10 "I'm happy from the inside out, and from the outside in, I'm firmly formed. 10 You canceled my ticket to hell—that's not my destination!" (Message).*

Father, I cancel today every grave dug for anyone in this church. I declare that no one will die in our midst in the name of Jesus!

334. *Isaiah 33:24 "No one in Zion will say, "I'm sick." Best of all, they'll all live guilt-free." (Message).*

Father, I declare that no one in this church family will say again, "I'm sick." We shall continue to enjoy divine health in the name of Jesus. No one shall suffer loss in KCCC in the name of Jesus!

335. *Psalms 126:4 Now, Lord, do it again! Restore us to our former glory! May streams of your refreshing flow over us until our dry hearts are drenched again. (Passion).*

Father, we declare restoration over all that has been stolen from us, in the name of Jesus. We declare that we recover all that has been taken from us; be it health, reputation, wealth, children, home, business, career, family, relationship, etc. We shout RESTORE, in the name of Jesus!

336. *Jeremiah 29: 11 1 "For I know the thoughts that I think toward you, says the LORD, thoughts of peace and not of evil, to give you a future and a hope."*

Father, in the name of Jesus, we claim peace and a spirit of refreshing for every heart here at this church that may have been broken in one way or another due to a failed relationship. Father, we claim total restoration and wholeness for every such situation. In the name of Jesus, we claim a future of divine expectation and eternal hope that comes only from your throne of grace, and we declare that all is well with our souls, in Jesus' name.

337. *3 John 1:2 "Dear friend, I'm praying that all is well with you and that you enjoy good health in the same way that you prosper spiritually." (CEB).*

Father, in the name of Jesus, restore sound health and wholeness to any member that may be challenged in their health. Let them enjoy supernatural strength and wholeness.

Victory

SINCE YOU ARE BORN OF GOD, YOU HAVE OVERCOME THE WORLD. YOUR FAITH IS THE VICTORY THAT HAS OVERCOME THE WORLD. "...THANKS BE TO GOD WHO GIVES US THE VICTORY THROUGH OUR LORD JESUS CHRIST." (I CORINTHIANS 15:57). LET US PRAY AS WE RECEIVE OUR VICTORY THROUGH FAITH IN EVERY AREA OF OUR LIVES. LET US PRAY!

338. *Isaiah 61:7 "Instead of shame and dishonor, you will enjoy a double share of honor. You will possess a double portion of prosperity in your land, and everlasting joy will be yours." (NLT).*

God, arise and fill my mouth with laughter, let my tears and shame expire, and let me possess a double portion of prosperity in this land, in the name of Jesus!

339. *Psalms 20: 5-6 "When you win, we plan to raise the roof and lead the parade with our banners. (Message).*

Father, lead us on a victory parade in this land and let everyone watch to see it. Send us the help you promised. Work and fill up all the gaps (financial, social, spiritual) in our lives, in the name of Jesus!

340. *Joshua 5:9 "Then the Lord said to Joshua, "This day I have rolled away the reproach of Egypt from you." (NKJV).*

Therefore, the name of the place is called, "Gilgal" to this day." Father, today roll away every reproach of my life, in the name of Jesus. Turn my tears to cheers, in the name of Jesus.

341. *Genesis 45:4-5 And Joseph said to his brothers, "Please come near to me." So they came near. Then he said: "I am Joseph your brother, whom you sold into Egypt. But now, do not therefore be grieved or angry with yourselves because you sold me here; for God sent me before you to preserve life. In the presence of those who think I'm nobody." (NKJV).*

Oh God, arise and make me somebody, in the name of Jesus!

342. *Hebrews 12:24 "to Jesus the Mediator of the new covenant, and to the blood of sprinkling that speaks better things than that of Abel." (NKJV).*

Father, let the blood of Jesus speak and release my destiny and prosperity from the altars and warehouses of evil foundation, in the mighty name of Jesus Christ!

343. *Deuteronomy 28: 6 "Wherever you go and whatever you do, you will be blessed." (NLT).*

As a church and as individuals, we declare that wherever we go, whatever we do, we will be blessed, we will be victorious, we will see godly results, and we will see righteous increase.

344. *Ephesians 2:13 "But now in Christ Jesus you who once were far off have been brought near by the blood of Christ." (NKJV).*

I use the blood of Jesus Christ to release and bring my destiny and glory from anywhere they have been buried, in the name of Jesus.

345. *Hebrews 10:19 "Therefore, brethren, having boldness to enter the Holiest by the blood of Jesus." (NKJV).*

By the blood of Jesus Christ, I speak destruction into the camp of my enemies. I crush the powers of evil altars and evil priesthood of my household, in the mighty name of Jesus Christ!

346. *Hebrews 13:20-21 "Now may the God of peace who brought up our Lord Jesus from the dead, that great Shepherd of the sheep, through the blood of the everlasting covenant, 21 make you [a]complete in every good work to do His will, working in [b]you what is well pleasing in His sight, through Jesus Christ, to whom be glory forever and ever. Amen." (NKJV).*

I receive wholeness in every area of my life, (physically, spiritually, financially, emotionally) by the blood of Jesus Christ!

347. *Revelation 12:11 "And they overcame him by the blood of the Lamb and by the word of their testimony, and they did not love their lives to the death." (NKJV).*

From now henceforth, I will begin to enjoy the realities of new creation in testimonies, and victories with fresh wind by the blood of Jesus Christ, in Jesus' mighty name!

348. *Ephesians 1:4 "Just as He chose us in Him before the foundation of the world, that we should be holy and without blame before Him in love." (NKJV).*

Therefore, I confess that I am born again because I have been chosen by Christ Jesus before the foundation of the world. No condemnation, no downcast, no contradiction, in the mighty name of Jesus!

349.   Hebrews 4:3" For we who have believed do enter that rest, as He has said: "So I swore in My wrath, 'They shall not enter My rest," although the works were finished from the foundation of the world." (NKJV).

Lord, I declare, in the name of Jesus Christ, that my deliverance from evil and idolatrous foundation has been finished from the foundation of the world. Father, I neutralize the claims and operations of evil and idolatrous foundation in my life, by the blood of Jesus Christ.

350.   1 Samuel 30:9-10 "David went, he and the six hundred men with him. They arrived at the Brook Besor, where some of them dropped out. David and four hundred men kept up the pursuit, but two hundred of them were too fatigued to cross the Brook Besor and stayed there." (Message).

Father, don't let me drop out in the battle of life. Let your Holy Spirit build me up and give me strength, in the name of Jesus. Give me strength to pray, to read the Word and walk in obedience to the WORD. Give me strength to be faithful in all areas of my life.

351.   Nehemiah 12:43 "Many sacrifices were offered on that joyous day, for God had given us cause for great joy. The women and children rejoiced, too, and the joy of the people of Jerusalem was heard far away!" (TLB).

Father, in the year 2015, give us reasons to rejoice and to celebrate. Let people come and celebrate with us in the name of Jesus.

352. *Romans 8:2 "For the law of the Spirit of life in Christ Jesus has made me free from the law of sin and death." (NKJV).*

My Lord, My King, I praise You for my freedom from sin and death.

353. *Psalm 8:4-5 "What is man that You are mindful of him, And the son of man that You visit him? For You have made him a little lower than the angels, And You have crowned him with glory and honor". (NKJV).*

Father, crown me with glory and honor. Everywhere I go, let people see your glory and honor upon my life.

354. *Isaiah 60:3 "The Gentiles shall come to your light, And kings to the brightness of your rising." (NKJV).*

Father, let every imprisoned and buried potential in me begin to come forth now, for the whole world to see, in the name of Jesus.

355. *Psalms 73:24 "You guide me with Your counsel, leading me to a glorious destiny." (NLT).*

Father, I declare, no matter the situation I am facing, I shall become what God has made me to be, in the name of Jesus!

356. *Revelation 3:11 "I'm on my way; I'll be there soon. Keep a tight grip on what you have so no one distracts you and steals your crown. (Message).*

Father, disgrace and destroy anything or anyone trying to distract me to steal my crown, my peace, my joy, or my relevance, in the name of Jesus!

357. *Psalms 73:24 "You guide me with Your counsel, leading me to a glorious destiny." (NLT).*

Father, I declare, no matter the situation I am facing, I shall become what God has made me to be, in the name of Jesus!

358. *Psalms 20: 5-6 "When you win, we plan to raise the roof and lead the parade with our banners. May all your wishes come true! That clinches it—help's coming, an answer is on the way, everything's going to work out." (Message).*

Father, lead us on a victory parade in this land and let everyone watch to see it. Send us the help you promised. Work and fill up all the gaps (financial, social, spiritual) in our lives, in the name of Jesus!

359. *Psalms 30:11 "You did it: you changed wild lament into whirling dance; You ripped off my black mourning band and decked me with wildflowers. (Message).*

Father, thank you for changing my stories from failure to success, sickness to health, debt to prosperity, lack to abundance, nobody to significance, and hate to celebrity, in the name of Jesus!

360. Psalms 26:4 *"I don't hang out with tricksters; I don't pal around with thugs (Message).*

Father, build walls of protection around me against tricksters and thugs, in the name of Jesus! Don't let me fall into their snares, in the name of Jesus!

361. 1 Samuel 17:54 *"And David took the head of the Philistine and brought it to Jerusalem, but he put his armor in his tent." (NKJV).*

O God, arise and place the head of my Goliath in my hands, in the name of Jesus!

362. Psalms 26:2 *"Examine me, God, from head to foot, order your battery of tests. Make sure I'm fit inside and out." (Message).*

Father, I declare that Your hand will perfect my life, in the name of Jesus! I will not live my life as a mess financially, spiritually, or physically, in the name of Jesus!

363. Psalms 26:7 *"Singing God-songs at the top of my lungs, telling God-stories." (Message).*

Father, I declare that I will sing songs of thanksgiving and I will tell of all your wonders in my life. My time to share testimonies has finally come, in the name of Jesus!

364. Psalms 20: 5-6 "When you win, we plan to raise the roof and lead the parade with our banners. May all your wishes come *true! 6 That clinches it—help's coming, an answer is on the way, everything's going to work out." (Message).*

Father, lead us on a victory parade in this land and let everyone watch to see it. Send us the help you promised. Work and fill up all the financial, social, and spiritual gaps in our lives, in the name of Jesus!

365. *Joshua 1:9 "This is my command—be strong and courageous! Do not be afraid or discouraged. For the Lord your God is with you wherever you go." (NLT).*

Father, manifest your presence in my life, home, children, work, finances, and in my health. Let my haters see you in my life and do not let the enemy rejoice over me, in the name of Jesus.

366. *Isaiah 30:19 "Oh yes, people of Zion, citizens of Jerusalem, your time of tears is over. Cry for help and you'll find it's grace and more grace. The moment He hears, He'll answer." (Message).*

Father, I declare that my tears are over, and my time of peace has arrived. Destiny helpers will locate me, and my family and we will enjoy favor every day, in the name of Jesus.

367. *Isaiah 54:14 "You'll be built solid, grounded in righteousness, far from any trouble—nothing to fear! far from terror—it won't even come close! (Message).*

Father, as we come to the end of this year, we declare that we are far from any trouble. Nothing will cause us to mourn, and we shall end this year in peace and prosperity, in the name of Jesus.

368. *Psalms 144: 1 "Praise the LORD, who is my rock. He trains my hands for war and gives my fingers skill for battle." (NLT).*

Father, we thank you for giving us victory in every battle we have fought this year. Thank you for making us winners and not losers, in the mighty name of Jesus.

369. *Psalms 33:12 "You have turned for me my mourning into dancing; You have put off my sackcloth and clothed me with gladness." (TPT).*

Father, we thank you for turning our mourning into dancing this year on this mountain. Thank you, for taking off our sack clothes and clothing us with gladness. Thank you for fighting our battles and giving us victory.

Blessing

"The lord will command the blessing on you in your storehouses and in all to which you set your hand, and He will bless you in the land which the lord your God is giving you." (DEUTERONOMY 28:8). You are not only blessed, you are also a blessing.

Let us pray the blessing!

370. Psalms 18:24 *"God rewrote the text of my life when I opened the book of my heart to his eyes." (Message).*

Father, rewrite the text of my life, fill in the details of your blessings and cancel every agenda of the wicked against me, my family, and this church, in the name of Jesus!

371. Deuteronomy 15:6 *"For the Lord your God will bless you just as He promised you; you shall lend to many nations, but you shall not borrow; you shall reign over many nations, but they shall not reign over you." (NKJV).*

Father, pour down your blessings on us. Establish the work of our hands. Make us lenders and not borrowers, rulers and not slaves over nations, in the name of Jesus!

372. Psalms 68:19 *"Blessed be The Lord, who daily loads us with benefits." (NKJV).*

Father, give us testimonies every day, at this church, for the glory of your name!

373. *Psalms 45:11 " So the King will greatly desire your beauty; Because He is your Lord, worship Him." (NKJV).*

Father, let your beauty reflect in my life, in my home, in my finances, and over my work, and let the World see it.

374. *Psalms 45:17 "I will make Your name to be remembered in all generations; Therefore, the people shall praise You forever and ever." (NKJV).*

Father, use me to the glory of your name and cause your power to manifest in my life, my home, my ministry, my work, in the name of Jesus.

375. *Psalms 68:28 "Summon your might; display your strength, O God, for you have done such mighty things for us." (TLB).*

Father, display your strength in my life, my home, my work, my ministry, and my family. Let me not be put to shame, yet stablish me for greatness, in the name of Jesus.

376. *Psalms 128: 5-6 "The Lord bless you out of Zion, and may you see the good of Jerusalem All the days of your life. Yes, may you see your children's children. Peace upon Israel!" (NKJV).*

Father, bless us out of Zion and let us, our children, and our children's children, see the good of our land all the days of our lives, in Jesus' Name.

377. *Psalms 115:14 "The LORD shall increase you more and more, you and your children." (NKJV).*

Father, increase this church more and more, in the name of Jesus! Increase us and our children more and more, and let the whole world see it.

378. 2 Chronicles 30:21 *"And in every work that he began in the service of the house of God, in the law and in the commandment, to seek his God, he did it with all his heart, so he prospered." (NKJV).*

Father, as we seek You and serve you with all our hearts at this church, prosper us and do not let our labor and service be in vain. Remember us for good, in the name of Jesus!

379. Psalms 18:24 *"God rewrote the text of my life when I opened the book of my heart to his eyes." (Message).*

Father, rewrite the text of my life, fill in the details of your blessings, and cancel every agenda of the wicked against me, my family, and this church, in the name of Jesus!

380. Psalms 75:1 *"Our God, we thank you for being so near to us! Everyone celebrates your wonderful deeds." (CEV).*

Father, we thank you for your blessings in our lives, children, homes, jobs, businesses, and church. Thank you for providing for our needs and for this new church building!

381. Revelation 3:13 *"Are your ears awake? Listen. Listen to the Wind Words, the Spirit blowing through the churches." (Message).*

Father, wake my ears up! Open my ears to listen and hear your voice. Don't let me go through life confused and defeated, in the name of Jesus!

382. *Deuteronomy 1:11 "May the Lord, the God of your ancestors, increase you a thousand times and bless you as He has promised!" (NKJV).*

Lord, increase this church a thousand times more and bless us, in the name of Jesus!

383. *Psalms 119:16 "Take my side as you promised; I'll live then for sure. Don't disappoint all my grand hopes." (Message).*

Father, bring to pass every promise you have given to me and cause me to give testimonies, in the name of Jesus!

384. *Psalm 119:170 "Give my request your personal attention, rescue me on the terms of your promise." (Message).*

Father, I declare that it is my turn to laugh and celebrate over my life, my home, my children, my business, my career, and my finances, in the name of Jesus!

385. *Micah 7:14 "O Lord, come and rule your people; lead your flock; make them live in peace and prosperity; let them enjoy the fertile pastures of Bashan and Gilead as they did long ago." (TLB).*

Father, lead us into prosperity, in the name of Jesus. Terminate financial struggle in our lives, in the name of Jesus! Open doors of advancement for us, in the name of Jesus!

386. *Exodus 36:5,7 "And they spoke to Moses, saying, "The people are bringing more than enough for doing this work that God has commanded us to do!" 7 There was plenty of material for all the work to be done. Enough and more than enough." (Message).*

Father, supply all the finances, materials and workers for the work of the new building. Let there be sufficiency and overflow, in the name of Jesus!

387. *Numbers 11:31 - And there went forth a wind from the LORD, and brought quails from the sea, and let them fall by the camp, as it were a day's journey on this side, and as it were a day's journey on the other side, round about the camp, and as it were two cubits high upon the face of the earth." (KJV).*

Father, let the wind from the Lord bring abundance to my life and terminate lack in my family, in the name of Jesus. Make me a blessing to my generation, in the name of Jesus!

388. *2 Chronicles 30:21 "And in every work that he began in the service of the house of God, in the law and in the commandment, to seek his God, he did it with all his heart, so he prospered." (NKJV).*

Father, as we seek You and serve you with all our hearts at this church, prosper us and do not let our labor and service be in vain. Remember us for good, in the name of Jesus!

389. *Psalm 27:3 "When besieged, I'm as calm as baby. When all hell broke loose, I'm collected and cool." (Message).*

Father, stabilize me physically, spiritually, and financially, and let nothing rob me of your peace in the name of Jesus! Steady my hands as I navigate through the journey of life, in the name of Jesus!

390. *Psalm 31:6 "I hate all this silly religion, but you, GOD, I trust." (Message).*

Father, reveal yourself to me and bring me into your inner circle. Don't let me run around in a silly religion that leads to no profit. Make my life an example of your goodness, in the name of Jesus.

391. *2 Chronicles 14:7 "…We have this peaceful land because we sought GOD; he has given us rest from all troubles." So, they built and enjoyed prosperity." (Message).*

Father, we declare peace and prosperity upon everyone that has given, and continues to give, to the building of this church's sanctuary. Let their hands always remain on top and let none of them suffer loss, in the name of Jesus!

392. *Numbers 11:31 - And there went forth a wind from the LORD, and brought quails from the sea, and let them fall by the camp, as it were a day's journey on this side, and as it were a day's journey on the other side, round about the camp, and as it were two cubits high upon the face of the earth." (KJV).*

Father, let the wind from the Lord bring abundance to my life and terminate lack in my family in the name of Jesus. Make me a blessing to my generation, in the name of Jesus!

393. *Psalm 119:173 "Put your hand out and steady me since I've chosen to live by your counsel." (Message).*

Father, reach out your hand and steady me and let nothing shake or destabilize me in my home and work, in the name of Jesus.

394. *Revelation 3:12 "Then I'll write names on you, the pillars: the Name of my God, the Name of God's City—the new Jerusalem coming down out of Heaven—and my new Name." (Message).*

Father, write new names on me, my spouse, my children and my church. Where we have been called sick, let them call us healed; where we have been called poor, let them call us rich; where we have been called ordinary, let them call us great!

395. *Psalms 90:13-14 "Come back, God—how long do we have to wait? —and treat your servants with kindness for a change. Surprise us with love at daybreak; then we'll skip and dance all day long." (Message).*

O Lord, make me a candidate of supernatural surprises, in favor, finances, and promotion, and launch me into my next level, in the name of Jesus!

396. *Esther 7:2 "And on the second day, at the banquet of wine, the king again said to Esther, "What is your petition, Queen Esther? It shall be granted you. And what is your request, up to half the kingdom? It shall be done!" (NKJV).*

Father, I declare that all my petitions receive speedy attention in heaven today. Grant me all that I requested in the name of Jesus. Let me share the testimony of your faithfulness in my life again, in the name of Jesus.

397. *Psalm 45:11 " So the King will greatly desire your beauty; Because He is your Lord, worship Him. (NKJV).*

Father, let your beauty be revealed in my life, in my home, in my children, in my finances, and over my work and let the world see it, in the name of Jesus!

398. *Isaiah 54:13 "All your children will be taught by the LORD, and they will have much peace. (NLT).*

Father, we declare that our children will receive revelation of your word, they will enjoy peace and be above only, in the name of Jesus.

399. *1 Samuel 28:15 "Why have you disturbed me by bringing me back?" Samuel asked Saul. "Because I am in deep trouble," he replied. "The Philistines are at war with us, and God has left me and won't reply by prophets or dreams; so, I have called for you to ask you what to do." (NLT).*

Father, cleanse me and purge me of anything and everything that can make me lose Your glorious presence. Lord, make Your presence more real to me day by day.

400. *Psalms 5:12 "For You, O Lord, will bless the righteous; with favor You will surround him as with a shield." (NKJV).*

Father, surprise me with favor this week, in the name of Jesus, and let your love surround me.

401. *1 Peter 1:5 "God is keeping careful watch over us and the future. The Day is coming when you'll have it all—life healed and whole. (Message).*

Father, let the great and prosperous future that you have for me begin today. Let my present show the preview of my future and make the whole world concur that your hand is upon my life, in the name of Jesus!

402. *James 5:11 "What a gift life is to those who stay the course! You've heard, of course, of Job's staying power, and you know how God brought it all together for him at the end. That's because God cares, cares right down to the last detail. (Message).*

Father, give me strength through your Holy Spirit to stay focused to the end. Make a gift out of my life and make my life a gift to my generation, and don't let my life end up in a mess. Take over my battle and work out the details of my life, in the name of Jesus!

403. *James 2:5 "Listen, dear friends. Isn't it clear by now that God operates quite differently? He chose the world's down-and-out as the kingdom's first citizens, with full rights and privileges. This kingdom is promised to anyone who loves God. (Message).*

Father, I decree and declare that from this day forward I will enjoy all the full rights and privileges of your kingdom's first citizens. I reject eating from life's leftovers, in the name of Jesus!

404. *Exodus 1:7 "But the children of Israel were fruitful and increased abundantly, multiplied and grew exceedingly mighty; and the land was filled with them." (NKJV).*

Father, we declare that we shall continue to be fruitful, and increase abundantly, in this land. We shall become exceedingly mighty and powerful. We shall possess the gates of the cities and make your glories known, in the name of Jesus.

405. *Nehemiah 13:14 "Remember me for what I have done, my God, and don't wipe out the good things that I have done for your temple and for the worship that is held there." (GW).*

Father, remember everyone giving to this ministry through their time, talents, and treasure. Don't wipe out the good things they have done in this house. Answer all their prayers speedily, in the name of Jesus.

Pastors

"Brethren, pray for us!" (I Thessalonians 5:25). This was a request from a leader of the people. Your Pastor needS your prayers, love them openly, pray for them secretly.

Apostle Paul requested again in Hebrews 13:18, "Pray for us, for we are confident that we have a good conscience, in all things desiring to live honorably." It is to our advantage that we pray for our pastors. Let us pray for NOT ONLY our Pastor, BUT pastors everywhere.

406. *Ecclesiastes 7:19 "Wisdom strengthens the wise more than ten rulers of the city." (NKJV).*

Father, strengthen our pastors and members of this church with wisdom and make us excel in all that we put our hands upon, in the name of Jesus!

407. *Luke 8:17 "For nothing is secret that will not be revealed, nor anything hidden that will not be known and come to light." (NKJV).*

Lord, bring to light and frustrate everything planned in darkness against our pastors and their family, in the name of Jesus!

408. *Ezekiel 34:5 "And they were scattered because there was no shepherd, and when they were scattered, they became food for all the wild beasts of the field." (Amplified).*

Father, destroy every organized network of demonic wickedness against our shepherds and pastors and their family; and render every negative utterance declared against them of no effect, in the name of Jesus!

409. *Joel 2:17 "Tell my servants, the priests, to cry inside the temple and to offer this prayer near the altar: "Save your people, LORD God! Don't let foreign nations make jokes about us. Don't let them laugh and ask, 'Where is your God?'" (CEV).*

Father, we declare that pastors and religious leaders will wake up to their duties of keeping the flock safe. Deliver our religious leaders from political pandering and turn their hearts towards the truth of your love. Open their eyes to understand their true calling, in the name of Jesus.

410. *Isaiah 61:6 6 You will be called priests of the LORD, ministers of our God. You will feed on the treasures of the nations and boast in their riches. (NLT).*

Father, we pronounce your blessings on pastors and religious leaders who have devoted themselves to the teaching of truth and love. Give them more insight to your Word, and provide for all their needs, in the name of Jesus.

411. *Zechariah 4:8-9, "Moreover the word of the Lord came to me, saying: "The hands of Zerubbabel Have laid the foundation of this temple; His hands shall also finish it. Then you will know That the Lord of hosts has sent Me to you. For who has despised the day of small things? For these seven rejoice to see." (NKJV).*

Father, we declare that the hands of your servants have started the building of the Temple, and their hands shall also finish it, in the name of Jesus.

412. *Isaiah 44: 24 -25 Thus says the Lord your Redeemer, And He who formed you from the womb: "I am the Lord who makes all things, who stretches out the heavens all alone; Who spreads abroad the earth by Myself; Who frustrates the signs of the babblers, and drives diviners mad; Who turns wise men backwards, And makes their knowledge foolishness." (NKJV).*

Father, in the name of Jesus, frustrate all the signs of the babblers and the wicked ones against our senior pastor, his wife, and the children; drive the diviners mad, turn the wise men backwards and make their knowledge become foolish. Protect them from the wicked ones, in Jesus' name.

413. *Psalms 128: 1-3 "Blessed is everyone who fears the Lord, Who walks in His ways. When you eat the labor of your hands, You shall be happy, and it shall be well with you. Your wife shall be like fruitful vine in the very heart of your house, Your children like olive plants all around your table." (NKJV).*

Father, teach us to walk in your fear and walk in your ways, so we can be happy when we eat the fruit of our labor in Jesus Name. Grant us peace and joy in our homes with our spouses and children, let us be fresh and flourishing to our old age, in Jesus' name.

414. *Job 5:12 "He frustrates the devices of the crafty, so that their hands cannot carry out their plans." (NKJV).*

Lord, build a wall of protection around our pastors and their children, in the name of Jesus. Let every plan against them be frustrated, in the name of Jesus!

415. *Isaiah 49:3 "And said unto me, Thou art my servant, O Israel, in whom I will be glorified." You are my dear servant in whom I will shine." (KJV).*

Father, in this year, empower the pastors, elders, and deacons of this church with Divine Wisdom, for greater results, and for the expansion of the kingdom of God at this church.

416. *2 Thessalonians 3:1 "Finally, brothers, pray for us, that the word of the Lord may spread rapidly and be glorified, even as also with you;" (New Heart English Bible).*

Father, through the ministry of your servant, the senior pastor of this church, let testimonies abound to your word in his mouth. Father, surround your servant, the senior pastor of this church, his wife, and their children with peace like a river; round-about, in this year.

417. *Luke 8:17 "For nothing is secret that will not be revealed, nor anything hidden that will not be known and come to light." (NKJV).*

Lord, bring to light everything planned in darkness against this church, its members, and our pastor's family, in the name of Jesus!

418. Acts 5:12 "And through the hands of the apostles many signs and wonders were done among the people. And they were all with one accord in Solomon's Porch. (NKJV).

Father, through the hands of your servants and our pastors, let many more signs and wonders be done among us. Increase their spiritual authority and influence all over the world, in the name of Jesus.

419. 1 Peter 2:4. "Welcome to the Living Stone, the source of life. The workmen took one look and threw it out; God set it in the place of honor." (Message).

Father, set our pastors up in the place of honor. Where they have been rejected, give them a place of honor there. Let those who have worked against them begin to work for them. Let those that hated them begin to celebrate them, in the name of Jesus!

420. Psalms 144:5, 7-8 "Step down out of heaven, God; ignite volcanoes in the hearts of the mountains...Reach all the way from sky to sea: pull me out of the ocean of hate, out of the grip of those barbarians. Who lie through their teeth, who shake your hand then knife you in the back." (Message).

Father, disgrace all who are incensed against our pastors, this church and every member of this church. In their presence make us your voice in this land and establish your presence in our midst in the name of Jesus!

421. 1 Chronicles 12:22 "Hardly a day went by without men showing up to help—it wasn't long before his band seemed as large as God's own army!" (Message).

Lord, bring more workers of Your choice to this church, make me a worker of your choice at this church. and keep all other evil agents away, in the name of Jesus!

422. *Psalms 27:6 "God holds me head and shoulders above all who try to pull me down..." (Message).*

Father, hold our pastors above all who try to pull them down, in the name of Jesus! Make their haters become irrelevant and confused, in the name of Jesus!

423. *Psalms 27:12 "Don't throw me to the dogs, those liars who are out to get me, filling the air with their threats." (Message).*

Father, preserve and protect our pastors and their family from those wicked liars and evil broadcasters. Return their evil imaginations against our pastors upon their heads, in the name of Jesus!

424. *Luke 10:19 "See what I've given you? Safe passage as you walk on snakes and scorpions, and protection from every assault of the Enemy. No one can put a hand on you!" (Message).*

Father, I praise you for keeping me, my family, my pastors, my church and all those surround me, safe since January. Thank you for keeping us safe from the attacks of the enemies and for granting us victory on every side in the name of Jesus!

425. *2 Chronicles 31:20 "Thus Hezekiah did throughout all Judah, and he did what was good and right and true before the LORD his God." (NKJV).*

Father, help us to always do what is good and right and true in your sight as we serve you here at this church. Do not let us lose relevance, in the name of Jesus!

426. Isaiah 61:6 *"You will be called priests of the Lord, ministers of our God. You will feed on the treasures of the nations and boast in their riches. (NLT).*

Father, we declare that our pastors and all who work in this church will continue to enjoy favor in your sight. They will feed on the treasures of the nations and will never lack, in the name of Jesus.

427. Psalms 35:8 *"Surprise them with your ambush— catch them in the very trap they set, the disaster they planned for me." (Message).*

Father, ambush those who plan against our pastors and their family. Catch those who plan against our senior pastor the very trap they set for him. Let their disastrous plan return to their heads, in the name of Jesus.

428. Psalms 35:4 *"When those thugs try to knife me in the back, make them look foolish. Frustrate all those who are plotting my downfall." (Message).*

Father, frustrate all those who are plotting the downfall of our senior pastor and their children, in the name of Jesus. Let all their haters look foolish and drain them of their strength, in the name of Jesus.

429. *Psalms 68:1-2 "God! Arise with awesome power, and every one of your enemies will scatter in fear! 2 Chase them away—all these God-haters. Blow them away as a puff of smoke. Melt them away like wax in the fire. One good look at you and the wicked vanish..." (Passion).*

Arise O God and scatter all the enemies of this church and let those who plan evil against this church and its members, be put to shame.

430. *Exodus 33:18 "Then Moses said, "Now, please show me your glory." (NCV).*

Father, manifest your glory in our midst at this church and pour out your Spirit in greater measure in our lives. May we encounter the manifestation of your presence, heavenly encounters, signs and wonders!

431. *Psalms 132:17 "I will increase the anointing that was upon David, and my glistening glory will rest upon my chosen ones. (Passion).*

Father, increase the anointing upon our pastors and let your glory rest upon them in the name of Jesus. Lord, perform unusual miracles through the hands of your servants, in the name of Jesus.

432. *Revelation 11:5 "If anyone attempts to harm them, fire will flow out of their mouths and consume their foes. All who seek to harm them will die in this way." (Passion).*

Father, we declare fire to come out of the mouth of our senior pastor and consume all who hate him, his family and this church. Let all who seek to harm him, his family, or this church, die in this way, in the name of Jesus.

433. Deuteronomy 33:11 *"Bless the ministry of the Levites, O LORD, and accept all the work of their hands. Hit their enemies where it hurts the most; strike down their foes so they never rise again." (NLT).*

Father, increase your blessing on the ministry of our senior pastor. Hit their enemies where it hurts the most. Lord, strike down all those who hate them, so they never rise again, in the name of Jesus.

434. Esther 9:3-4 *"What's more, all the government officials, satraps, governors—everyone who worked for the king—actually helped the Jews because of Mordecai; they were afraid of him. 4 Mordecai by now was a power in the palace. As Mordecai became more and more powerful, his reputation had grown in all the provinces." (Message).*

Father, make our senior pastor a power in this land. Establish him as your voice and make government officials, governors, senators and business communities come to him for advice. Give him a name that no one can destroy, in the name of Jesus.

435. 1 Samuel 5:11 *"The people summoned the Philistine rulers again and begged them, "Please send the Ark of the God of Israel back to its own country, or it will kill us all." For the deadly* *plague from God had already begun, and great fear was sweeping across the town." (NLT).*

Father, we command deadly plague from God over the enemies of our pastors, and their family. Frustrate all the haters of our senior pastor and their children, in the mighty name of Jesus Christ! Lord, let the fear of our senior pastor sweep across those who hate him and make him rulers over them, in the mighty name of Jesus!

436. *Psalm 71: 21 "You shall increase my greatness, And comfort me on every side." (NKJV).*

Father, increase the greatness of our senior pastor and make him comfortable on every side in the mighty name of Jesus! Strengthen Your servant, honor him, and bless him with every good blessing of Your love.

437. *2 Kings 19:34 "For I will defend this city, to save it, for mine own sake, and for my servant David's sake." (KJV).*

We declare by the Word of the Lord, Father, defend the family of our senior pastor by reason of your son' s obedience to your call. Defend his home!

438. *Proverbs 31:25 "Strength and honor are her clothing; And she shall rejoice in time to come." (KJV).*

Father, we declare concerning our senior pastor's wife, that the days of her rejoicing have come!

439. *Isaiah 43:1-2 "But now, says the Lord the one who created you, Jacob, the one who formed you, Israel: Don't fear, for I have redeemed you; I have called you by name; you are mine. When you pass through the waters, I will be with you; when through the rivers, they won't sweep over you. When you walk through the fire, you won't be scorched and the flame won't burn you." (CEB).*

Father, thank you for rescuing our senior pastor, his wife, and their children from the hand of the enemy. Now, let your presence be with them. When they pass through water, they will not get drowned. When they walk through fire, they will not be scorched, in the mighty name of Jesus Christ!

440. *Isaiah 43:4 "Because you are precious in my eyes, you are honored, and I love you. I give people in your place, and nations in exchange for your life." (Amplified).*

Father, according to your word, our senior pastor, his wife and their children are precious in your eyes. Honor them. Give people in their place and nations in exchange for their life, in the mighty name of Jesus Christ.

441. *Matthew 4:16 "The people which sat in darkness saw great light; and to them which sat in the region and shadow of death light is sprung up." (KJV).*

Father, by the power of your Word coming from this church's altar, command major transformations across the globe, kindle major revival fire in the life of men and women all around the world!

442. *2 Thessalonians 3:1 "Finally, dear brothers and sisters, we ask you to pray for us. Pray that the Lord's message will spread rapidly and be honored wherever it goes, just as when it came to you." (NLT).*

Father, in the name of Jesus, let the message you gave your servant, our senior pastor, spread rapidly and be honored in signs and wonders wherever it goes.

443. *Deuteronomy 34:7 "Moses was a hundred and twenty years old when he died, yet his eyes were not weak, and his vitality had not diminished." (Berean Study Bible).*

Father, in the name of Jesus, continue to increase the strength of your servant, our senior pastor, and his family on every side. As their days go, so let their strength increase.

Success

The Lord was with Joseph, and he was successful in the land of Egypt. God has built success into our DNA. You shall be like a tree planted by the rivers of water, that brings forth its fruit in its season, whose leaf also shall not wither, and whatever he does shall prosper. Success is your portion. Let us pray your success.

444. Psalms 69:13 *"But I keep right on praying to you, Lord. For now, is the time--you are bending down to hear! You are ready with a plentiful supply of love and kindness. Now answer my prayer and rescue me as you promised." (TLB).*

Father, bring to pass every promise you have given to me, and cause me to give testimonies, in the name of Jesus.

445. Nehemiah 12:43 *"Many sacrifices were offered on that joyous day, for God had given us cause for great joy. The women and children rejoiced, too, and the joy of the people of Jerusalem was heard far away!" (TLB).*

Father, in this year, give us reasons to rejoice and to celebrate. Let people come and celebrate with us, in the name of Jesus.

446. Psalms 118:25 *"Save now, I pray O Lord; O Lord, I pray, send now prosperity." (NKJV).*

Lord, send prosperity to this church and its members, in the name of Jesus! Let no one be missing!

447. *Daniel 1:17-20 "As for these four young men, God gave them knowledge and skill in all literature and wisdom; and Daniel had understanding in all visions and dreams. And in all matters of wisdom and understanding about which the king examined them, he found them ten times better than all the magicians and astrologers who were in all his realm." (NKJV).*

Father, I receive access to supernatural knowledge and skill for my career and my business. Starting today, I am the best in what I do, in the name of Jesus. I know how to achieve excellent results with minimal resources, without sweat.

448. *Isaiah 48:16-17 "Come near to Me, hear this: I have not spoken in secret from the beginning; From the time that it was, I was there. And now the Lord God and His Spirit Have sent Me." Thus says the Lord, your Redeemer, The Holy One of Israel: "I am the Lord your God, Who teaches you to profit, Who leads you by the way you should go." (NKJV).*

Father, I declare that all my business operations and career activities come under the FRESH ANOINTING of the Holy Spirit for supernatural profits and wealth creation!

449. *Deuteronomy 1:11 "May the Lord, the God of your ancestors, increase you a thousand times and bless you as He has promised!" (NIV).*

Lord, increase this church a thousand times more and bless us in the name of Jesus!

450. *Deuteronomy 30:9 "Then the Lord your God will make you most prosperous in all the work of your hands and in the fruit of* your womb, the young of your livestock and the crops of your land...." (NIV).

Father, let my hands carry the anointing for prosperity, in the name of Jesus!

451. Psalms 90:17 "May the favor of the Lord our God rest on us; establish the work of our hands for us—yes, establish the work of our hands." (NIV).

Favor, envelope my life, in the name of Jesus! Divine favor, envelope my life, in the name of Jesus!

452. Isaiah 40:29 "He gives power to the faint and weary, and to him who has no might He increases strength [causing it to multiply and making it to abound." (Amplified).

Father, I declare that what has taken other people many years to achieve, I will achieve in a few months, in the name of Jesus!

453. 2 Chronicles 29:36 "Hezekiah and all the people rejoiced at what God had brought about for his people, because it was done so quickly". (NIV).

Father, I receive divine acceleration in my life, in the name of Jesus!

454. Psalms 90:13-14 "Come back, God—how long do we have to wait? —and treat your servants with kindness for a change. Surprise us with love at daybreak; then we'll skip and dance all day long." (Message).

Lord, make me a candidate of supernatural surprises, in favor, finances, and promotion and launch me into my next level, in the name of Jesus!

455. *Psalms 73:24 "You guide me with Your counsel, leading me to a glorious destiny." (NLT).*

Father, I declare, no matter the situation I am facing, I shall become what God has made me to be, in the name of Jesus!

456. *Psalms 115: 14-15 "May the Lord richly bless both you and your children. 15. May you be blessed by the Lord, who made heaven and earth." (NLT).*

Father, I declare, this year, I shall be blessed with unrivaled lifting, and I shall be celebrated, in the name of Jesus!

457. *Psalms 69:13 "But I keep right on praying to you, Lord. For now, is the time--you are bending down to hear! You are ready with a plentiful supply of love and kindness. Now answer my prayer and rescue me as you promised." (TLB).*

Father, bring to pass every promise you have given to me and cause me to give testimonies, in the name of Jesus.

458. *Psalms 108:13 Through God we will do valiantly, for it is He who shall tread down our enemies. (NKJV).*

Father, this year we shall do valiantly in our finances, homes, business, ministry, education, and church. I destroy every power preventing me from moving forward, in the name of Jesus!

459. *James 5:11 "What a gift life is to those who stay the course! You've heard, of course, of Job's staying power, and you know how God brought it all together for him at the end. That's because God cares, cares right down to the last detail." (Message).*

Father, give me strength through your Holy Spirit to stay focused to the end. Make a gift out of my life and make my life a gift to my generation. Don't let my life end up in a mess. Take over my battle and work out the details of my life, in the name of Jesus!

460. *James 2:5 "Listen, dear friends. Isn't it clear by now that God operates quite differently? He chose the world's down-and-out as the kingdom's first citizens, with full rights and privileges. This kingdom is promised to anyone who loves God." (Message).*

Father, I decree and declare that from this day forward I will enjoy all the full rights and privileges of your kingdom's first citizens. I reject eating from life's leftovers, in the name of Jesus!

461. *Psalms 45:11 "So the King will greatly desire your beauty; Because He is your Lord, worship Him." (NKJV).*

Father, let your beauty reflect in my life, in my home, in my finances and over my work, and let the World see it.

462. *Psalms 119:16 "Take my side as you promised; I'll live then for sure. Don't disappoint all my grand hopes." (Message).*

Father, bring to pass every promise you have given to me and cause me to give testimonies, in the name of Jesus!

463. *Psalms 119:170 "Give my request your personal attention, rescue me on the terms of your promise." (Message).*

Father, I declare that it is my turn to laugh and celebrate over my life, my home, my children, my business, my career, and my finances, in the name of Jesus!

464. *Psalms 119:170 "Give my request your personal attention, rescue me on the terms of your promise." (Message).*

Father, bring to pass every promise you have given to me and cause me to give testimonies, in the name of Jesus!

465. *Micah 7:14 "O Lord, come and rule your people; lead your flock; make them live in peace and prosperity; let them enjoy the fertile pastures of Bashan and Gilead as they did long ago." (TLB).*

Father, lead us into prosperity, in the name of Jesus. Terminate financial struggle in our lives in the name of Jesus! Open doors of advancement for us, in the name of Jesus!

466. *Psalms 90:13-14 "Come back, God—how long do we have to wait? —and treat your servants with kindness for a change. 14 Surprise us with love at daybreak; then we'll skip and dance all day long."(Message).*

O Lord, I declare that I am a candidate of supernatural surprises, in favor, finances, and promotion and launch me into my next level, in the name of Jesus!

467. *Psalms 115: -15 "May the Lord richly bless both you and your children. 15 May you be blessed by the Lord, who made heaven and earth." (NLT).*

Father, I declare, this year, I shall be blessed with unrivaled lifting, and I shall be celebrated, in the name of Jesus!

468. *Psalms 69:29-30 "But rescue me, O God, from my poverty and pain. Then I will praise God with my singing! My thanks will be his praise." (TLB).*

Father, rescue me from poverty and pain. Let favor locate me and terminate labor and toiling in my life, in the name of Jesus.

469. *Psalms 1:3 "They are like trees growing beside a stream, trees that produce fruit in season and always have leaves. Those people succeed in everything they do." (CEV).*

Father, I am planted in your house, let me produce fruit in season, and do not let my leaves dry. Keep me fresh by the power of your word, in the name of Jesus.

470. *Job 41:11 "I am in command of the world and in debt to no one." (CEV).*

Father, I declare myself free from financial burden and debt, in the name of Jesus. God of abundance, I receive supernatural abundance of your provision to become a blessing to others around me, in the name of Jesus.

471. *Proverbs 4:18 says, "The path of the just is like a shining light, that shines brighter and brighter to the perfect day." (NKJV).*

Father, I declare that I will finish this year with joy and not with sadness, in the name of Jesus! I will finish this year on the positive financially, in the name of Jesus!

472. *Psalms 85:6 "Why not help us make a fresh start—a resurrection life? Then your people will laugh and sing!" (Message).*

Father, press the reset button and give us a fresh encounter with you this year. No more stale songs, but give us a new song this year, in the name of Jesus!

473. *Psalms 92: 12-13 "The righteous shall flourish like a palm tree, He shall grow like a cedar in Lebanon. Those who are planted in the house of the LORD Shall flourish in the courts of our God." (NKJV).*

Father, we pray that everyone connected to this church's family shall grow and flourish in health, finances, relationships, and businesses, in Jesus' name.

Made in United States
Troutdale, OR
09/04/2023

12640828R00086